Gospel of John

The Word IN **LIFE**™ *Study Bible*

THOMAS NELSON PUBLISHERS
Nashville

ACKNOWLEDGMENTS

John 4:48: "Ten Myths About Christianity, Myth #3: Science Is In Conflict with Christian Faith." Adapted by permission from *Ten Myths About Christianity* by Michael Green and Gordon Carkner, Lion Publishing, 1988.

John 5:17: "God—The Original Worker." Adapted by permission from Doug Sherman and William Hendricks, *Your Work Matters to God*, NavPress, 1987.

John 15:18–20: quotation from A. W. Tozer, *A Treasury of A. W. Tozer*, Baker Book House, 1980.

John 18:37–38: quotation reprinted from *Walking on Water* by Madeleine L'Engle, ©1980 by Crosswicks. Used by permission of Harold Shaw Publishers, Wheaton, Ill.

ABOUT THIS EDITION OF THE GOSPEL OF JOHN

This special edition of **The Word In Life Study Bible, Gospel of John,** *is intended to help you get to know Jesus. No one else in history has had as much effect on how people think and act. Apart from Him, Christianity—even life itself—would make no sense.*

Many books, movies and people try to convey some image of Jesus to our culture.

On the following pages are the writings of John, one of the original followers of Jesus. Included with John's eyewitness account are special articles and study aids to help you further explore Jesus and His mission.

Knowing Jesus is essential to understanding Christianity—and it may become an exciting lifelong adventure for you.

THE GOSPEL SHOWS THAT KNOWING *ABOUT* GOD IS NOT THE SAME AS *KNOWING* GOD

Many people have knowledge about religion, Christianity, and the Bible. But intellectual knowledge is not the same as vital faith. Knowing **about** *God is not the same as having a personal relationship with Him.*

This is clear from everyday relationships. Reading books on marriage is not the same as spending time with one's spouse. Knowing someone's phone number is a far cry from enjoying friendship with that person.

In the same way, *knowing* God involves far more than knowing *about* Him. Information alone does not produce real faith. To be sure, right thinking is involved in faith, but faith is more than mere knowledge. For example, John often mentioned Jewish leaders who knew quite a bit about the Scriptures, religious rules and faith in God (John 5:10; 6:30, 31). Jesus warned these leaders that knowing the truth about God involved more than thinking; it meant *doing* God's will (John 7:14–24). Spiritual insight and vitality involve action.

Are you a believer in need of spiritual renewal? What disciplines might help you get started on making your faith vital once again? Perhaps you might:

- Establish a small group with others in your workplace, industry, neighborhood, or family to meet regularly for prayer and discussion about how Christ enters into everyday situations.

- Volunteer for a program to serve the needy through your church or a community service agency.

- Speak out on school or workplace policies, decisions, or practices that you know to be unethical or harmful to others or the environment.

- Begin a regular habit of Bible reading and study in order to apply God's Word to your life.

- Begin patterns of prayer such as: prayer for people with whom you live and work—even those you may not like; prayers of thanksgiving for the things God has done for you and for the responsibilities He has given to you; prayers of confession and repentance for sin or areas of neglect in your life; prayers that meditate on God and His Word; prayers that express your innermost feelings and thoughts to God.

- Keep a journal of developments and changes in your life.

- Take on a task that uses an ability with which God has gifted you, especially if that ability is unused or underused elsewhere in your life.

- Consider whether you have ignored, offended or hurt someone and need to repent of your error and apologize to that person.

The point is, faith works best when it is the central unifying factor in one's life. Christ must never be just one more thing to occasionally acknowledge; rather, He must be the Lord of life and be brought into every area of life. ◆

JOHN'S GOSPEL HELPS TO IDENTIFY JESUS AND HIS MISSION

John wrote his Gospel to communicate particular information about Jesus. He carefully structured his writing around a series of seven signs. See the article and chart in the Introduction to John's Gospel.

John also included a series of **metaphors,** symbols, that Jesus used to reveal His mission and unique identity. Each of the metaphors begins with Jesus' words "I am" and then links Jesus to a common but essential character or item in the world of that day. As you look at each of the statements, consider what each meant to the people who first heard Jesus use the metaphor, and apply Jesus' claim in your own situation. ◆

THE "I AM" STATEMENTS

"I am the bread of life" (6:35)
The source of essential things

"I am the light of the world" (8:12)
The means of finding direction

"I am the door of the sheep" (10:7)
The way in and out, of belonging

"I am the good shepherd" (10:14)
The one who loves and cares

"I am the resurrection and the life" (11:25)
The way to permanence

"I am the way, the truth, and the life" (14:6)
The source of relationship with God

"I am the true vine" (15:1)
The means of productivity

THE BIBLE CALLS JESUS BY MANY NAMES THAT REVEAL HIS IDENTITY

THE NAMES OF JESUS

Jesus is identified in Scripture by many different names and titles. These indicate numerous aspects of His nature, character and roles. You may want to look up some of these passages to get to know Jesus better.

Name or Title	Description
Adam (1 Cor. 15:45)	The first Adam brought death through sin; Jesus, "the last Adam," brought life through His righteousness.
The Alpha and the Omega (Rev. 21:6)	Jesus is eternal, "the Beginning and the End." Alpha is the first letter in the Greek alphabet, omega is the last.
Apostle (Heb. 3:1)	"Messenger." Jesus came to bring the good news of salvation to humanity.
The bread of life (John 6:35, 48)	Jesus is the heavenly manna, the spiritual food, given by the Father to those who ask for it.
The chief cornerstone (Eph. 2:20)	Jesus is the foundation of the church.
The Chief Shepherd (1 Pet. 5:4)	The title that Peter called Jesus, indicating His oversight of His "flock," the church.
The Christ (Matt. 1:1, 17; 16:16; Luke 2:11; John 1:40)	From the Greek word *Christos,* "Messiah" or "Anointed One." Jesus fulfills the Old Testament promise of a Messiah.
The Consolation of Israel (Luke 2:25)	Jesus came to bring comfort to the nation (Is. 40:1–2).

Continued

Name or Title	Description
The firstborn from the dead (Col. 1:18)	Jesus overcame death in order to give life to believers.
The firstborn over all creation (Col. 1:15)	As God's Son, Jesus rules over everything that exists.
The good shepherd (John 10:11, 14; compare Heb. 13:20)	An image that Jesus used to describe His relationship to His people.
The head of the body, the church (Eph. 1:22–23; 4:15–16; Col. 1:18)	Jesus is the leader of His people and the source of their life.
High Priest (Heb. 3:1)	Like the Old Testament high priest, Jesus stands between God and people to offer an acceptable sacrifice for sin.
The Holy One of God (Mark 1:24; John 6:69)	Jesus is the sinless Messiah promised by God.
I AM (John 8:58)	A name by which God made Himself known to Moses (Ex. 3:14), related to the verb "to be."
The image of the invisible God (Col. 1:15)	Jesus expresses God in bodily form.
Immanuel (Matt. 1:23)	"God with us" (Is. 7:14).
Jesus (Matt. 1:21; Luke 1:30; Acts 9:5)	The name that God instructed Joseph and Mary to call their Son.
King of Kings and Lord of Lords (Rev. 19:16)	The formal title that Jesus has received, indicating His supremacy as the one to whom "every knee should bow" (Phil. 2:9–11).
King of the Jews (Matt. 2:2; 27:11–12; John 19:19)	As Messiah, Jesus is Israel's king, fulfilling God's promises to David (2 Sam. 7:12–16).
The Lamb of God (John 1:29, 35)	Jesus became the atoning sacrifice for sin.
The light of the world (John 9:5)	Jesus brings truth and hope to light in the midst of spiritual darkness.
Lord (Luke 2:11; 1 Cor. 2:8; Phil. 2:11)	A title indicating ultimate sovereignty.
Mediator between God and men (1 Tim. 2:5)	Jesus reestablishes the relationship between God and people.
The only Begotten of the Father (John 1:14)	Jesus is God's only Son.
The Prophet (Mark 6:15; John 7:40; Acts 3:22)	Jesus is the leader that God promised to "raise up" like Moses (Deut. 18:15, 18–19).
Rabbi (John 1:38; 3:2)	Friends and enemies alike recognized Jesus as Teacher.
Savior (Luke 1:47; 2:11)	Jesus came to save people from their sins.
Seed (of Abraham; Gal. 3:16)	God made promises to Abraham and his "Seed," whom Paul identified as Christ (Gen. 13:15; 17:8).
The Son of Abraham (Matt. 1:1)	Jesus descended from Abraham and fulfills the promises of God to Abraham (Gen. 22:18).
The Son of David (Matt. 1:1)	Jesus descended from David and fulfills the promises of God to David (2 Sam. 7:12–16).
The Son of God (John 1:24; 9:35–37)	Jesus is one of three Persons of the Trinity (Father, Son, and Holy Spirit).
The Son of Man (Matt. 18:11; John 1:51)	Though fully God, Jesus took on a human body (compare Phil. 2:5–8).
The Word (John 1:1; Rev. 19:13)	Jesus is fully God and therefore is the full expression of God.

JOHN'S GOSPEL SHOWS US RESPONSES TO JESUS

According to John (and the other New Testament writers), Jesus was not the kind of person people could easily ignore. Wherever Jesus went people noticed Him. He touched people from all walks of life. From the very poor (such as the paralyzed man of John 5:2–15) to the very rich (such as the nobleman of John 4:46–54), people responded to Jesus because He could meet their needs.

The powerless (such as the Samaritan woman of John 4:5–42) and the influential (such as Caiphas, John 11:45–52 and 18:12–28) sometimes found themselves forced to respond to Jesus against their choice. Then there were the disciples, who followed Jesus because He had words of eternal life (John 6:68). The crowds were fascinated by Jesus but sometimes found His teaching too hard to follow (John 6:60–67). The religious leaders were threatened by Jesus and often fought with Him (see the article at John 8:48).

Andrew, Nicodemus, Martha, Lazarus, Pilate and Mary Magdalene are just a few of the different people who encounter Jesus in the Gospel of John. Many of the people featured in John's Gospel faced situations similar to the ones we face today. Like us, they were concerned about finding the truth, and had needs they wanted someone to meet. Perhaps they had made mistakes and were seeking a way out, or were concerned about their place in the world.

People's responses to Jesus ranged from adoring worship to fearful contempt. Often, their preconceived ideas about God or the Messiah heavily influenced their responses. Some were afraid of the changes Jesus might cause in their lives. Others were looking for something He might be able to give them. Some were surprised to encounter someone like Jesus at all. Many responded in faith and followed Jesus. What will *your* response be?

As you read through the Gospel of John, look for characters who are in situations similar to your own. Then ask yourself if Jesus has the ability or power to address *your* situation. ◆

JOHN'S GOSPEL REVEALS JESUS' RESPONSE TO YOU

What does Jesus want for you?

Relationships usually involve giving and receiving. When two people enter into a loving relationship, they often have ideas about what they can give each other. In John's Gospel we get a picture of some of the things Jesus wants for those who follow Him. In John 17, Jesus prays for His disciples and mentions those who will become His followers in the future. His prayer reveals what He wants for all of His disciples. Below are listed some of the things mentioned; you may find others as you read through John. Are they the kind of things that interest you as well?

- Eternal Life (17:2)
- Security (17:11)
- Joy (17:13)
- The Word of God (17:14)
- Protection from Evil (17:15)
- Holiness or Purity (17:16)
- Truth (17:17)
- Unity (17:21)
- Glory (17:22)
- Experience of Love (17:23) ◆

JOHN'S GOSPEL SPEAKS OUT ON ISSUES RELEVANT TO OUR WORLD

Does Jesus' teaching speak in relevant ways to the issues of our day? John tells us how Jesus acted in response to social, political and religious issues in the first century. Some of the issues today are very similar.

Use this table as a starting point for your own study of the issues. Examine the articles mentioned, and the statements in John's Gospel. Apply what you learn to your everyday life. ◆

JOHN	
Race and Ethnicity	•Jesus refused to play ethnic games when there was a matter of eternal life and death at stake. See "Ethnic Games with Religious Roots," John 4:19–23.
The Church	•To be effective, believers must remain "on line" with Jesus, drawing from His resources and obeying His commands. See "The Network," John 15:1–10. •John records a prayer of Jesus that shows that engagement with the world, not isolation, is His desire for His church. See "Called Into the World," John 17:18.
Laity	•Have you ever struggled with doubts or tough questions about Christ, the Christian faith, or the church? See "Skeptics Welcome," John 20:24–31.
Witness	•John presents back-to-back accounts that show two of the many different ways in which Jesus dealt with people. See "The Gospel in a Pluralistic Society," John 3:21. •One thing is certain about evangelism: both non-Christians and Christians feel uncomfortable with it. See "Whose Job Is Evangelism?" John 16:8.
Gender	•An attempt to humiliate a woman before Jesus results in His setting a new standard for judgment. See "A Double Standard," John 8:2–3.
Public Systems	•John's Gospel presents another man named John whose behavior seems to repudiate the common measures of success in our society. See "Success," John 3:30.
Work	•A statement by Jesus shows that God is a worker who continues to maintain the creation and provide for His creatures. See "God—The Original Worker," John 5:17.
The City	•Jesus tapped into one of the most powerful concepts of the Old Testament—the idea that a specific place on earth is made special because of God's presence there. See "Sacred Space," John 1:51.

•　•

DISCOVER JESUS IN THE GOSPEL OF JOHN

After considering the questions and challenges discussed above, read through *The Word In Life Study Bible, Gospel of John.* At a pace that is comfortable for you, read the entire Gospel, pausing to consider the ideas raised in the supplementary materials. As you see how Jesus touched the lives of others, and He becomes more real to you, perhaps you'll discover what His plan is for *your* life. ◆

CONTENTS

INTRODUCTION

This edition of John's Gospel is part of *The Word In Life Study Bible,* the beginning of a new generation of study Bibles. Its purpose is to help you discover ways to relate the Word of God to you and the world you live in. This Bible makes it easy to bring the Word into your own world by taking you right into the world of the Bible.

The Word In Life Study Bible helps you get a clear understanding of God's Word by focusing on the surroundings of the biblical narrative. Stimulating articles get you thinking about how to relate the teachings of God's Word to life. The articles raise questions about what it means to live for God in today's world—about what a believer's role in the world is—and about how the Word in one life can touch the lives of others.

Features about the people, places, and customs of Jesus' world make the teachings of the Bible more vivid. You'll find friends in the Word of God. You'll feel at home where they lived. You'll discover that people aren't much different now than they were two thousand years ago. And you'll see that God's Word is more useful than you ever realized.

Explore the following pages and take a closer look at *The Word In Life Study Bible*—what it's meant to do, what it looks like, and how it works.

WHY THIS KIND OF PUBLICATION?

Someone has well said that Scripture was not written merely to be studied, but to change our lives. Likewise, James exhorts us to be "doers of the word, and not hearers only" (James 1:22). And Jesus said, "By this My Father is glorified, that you bear much fruit; so you will be my disciples" (John 15:8). Clearly, the point of God's Word is not to make us "smarter sinners" but to help us become more like Jesus Christ by making the Word of God part of our lives.

However, applying biblical truth in this day and age is far from easy. In the first place, the fact that the Bible was written thousands of years ago in a different culture can sometimes make it difficult to understand. And even if we grasp what the writers were saying to their original readers, we still must make the connection to our own situation today. In the end, many people wonder: can Scripture really make any difference in our complex, modern world? Yes it can, and this publication helps to show the way. ◆

A "USER-FRIENDLY" STUDY BIBLE

THE WORD IN LIFE STUDY BIBLE HELPS YOU UNDERSTAND THE BIBLICAL TEXT.

Before you can apply Scripture, you must understand what Scripture means. That's why The Word In Life Study Bible provides the kind of information you'll need to make sense of what the biblical text is talking about. The articles and other information (see below) provide the "who, what, when, where, how, and why" behind scores of passages, in an interesting, easy-to-understand way. Not only do they offer insight into the text, they also help you to understand the context of those passages, so that you can connect the words and events of biblical times with today.

THE WORD IN LIFE STUDY BIBLE HELPS YOU APPLY SCRIPTURE TO EVERYDAY LIFE.

"Wow! This is the kind of Bible I need in my life," one reader said. "It just makes Scripture come alive. It's contemporary. It's relevant." As you read The Word In Life Study Bible, you won't have to search and struggle for ways to apply God's Word; the articles suggest numerous possibilities for how Scripture makes a difference. That's especially helpful if you're one who is strapped for time or likes to quickly get to the point.

THE WORD IN LIFE STUDY BIBLE CHALLENGES YOU TO DEVELOP YOUR OWN THINKING.

You won't find pat answers or a "packaged" theology in this study Bible. Instead, the articles are designed to provoke your thinking by relating the text of Scripture to the issues of today, providing information to guide your thinking. Sometimes the commentary will raise a question without answering it; sometimes it will suggest possible answers. Often it will point out things that you may not have considered before. The articles don't pretend to address every issue raised by the biblical text or to solve every theological problem. But they're guaranteed to make you think!

THE WORD IN LIFE STUDY BIBLE INTRODUCES YOU TO THE PEOPLE OF SCRIPTURE.

For too many readers, the Bible can seem dull and lifeless, a book that only scholars and mystics might find interesting. But Scripture comes alive once we discover the people in the text. The Word In Life Study Bible is designed to help you do that, to "make friends" with some of the fascinating characters that God chose to include in His Word. They receive special attention through "Personality Profiles" that summarize what we know of them (see below). Even though these people lived long ago, you'll find that you have far more in common with them than you have differences. They experienced many of the same things you do. By learning what God did in their lives, you'll gain insight into what God is doing in yours.

THE WORD IN LIFE STUDY BIBLE MAKES THE BIBLE EASY TO READ.

"I know I should read the Bible more, but to be honest, I just don't have time!" Have you ever felt that way? If so, The Word In Life Study Bible is for you. It was designed for busy people. In the first place, you'll enjoy how easy it is to read the New King James Version. A modern translation that preserves the stylistic beauty of the King James Version, the NKJV presents the eternal Word of God in everyday language that people can understand. You'll also find the material presented in bite-size units, with section headings to mark the text. The Scriptures are accompanied not by long, drawn out treatises, but by straight-to-the-point articles and other information presented in simple, easily grasped terms. ◆

FEATURES TO LOOK FOR

INTRODUCTORY ARTICLES

At the beginning of a book of the Bible you'll find information that explains why the book is important and what to pay attention to as you read it. You'll learn something of the background behind the book, including who the author and original readers were. You'll also get an idea of the issues the book addresses through a table of contents that describes some of the articles you'll find alongside the text.

CONSIDER THIS

As mentioned above, God intended His Word to change people's lives. That's why occasionally you'll find a symbol that refers you to a nearby article relating in some way to the text indicated. These articles help to explain the Scriptural passages and highlight the significance of biblical truths for modern readers. In articles with this symbol, ways are offered for you to consider how the passage applies to your life and the world around you.

FOR YOUR INFO

This symbol indicates articles that primarily offer information about the text or its cultural context. Knowing the background of a biblical passage will help you understand it more accurately and make it more useful to you.

PERSONALITY PROFILES

One of the goals that the editors of The Word In Life Study Bible *had in developing their material was to introduce readers to the people of the Scriptures, including those who lived and worked in public places. One of the important ways that this study Bible does that is through personality profiles that highlight various individuals. These are not biographies, but summaries of what the Bible tells us about the person, what can be reasonably inferred from the text, and what other sources report about his or her life and legacy.*

YOU ARE THERE

One of the most important windows on understanding the text of Scripture is knowing the places where the events occurred. Unfortunately, ancient localities are unknown to most modern readers. The cities of Acts, for example, are little more than dots on a map for most of us. Yet when we examine the geography of the New Testament, we discover that the first-century Roman world was quite a bit like our own. The articles indicated by the "you are there" symbol will take you to places that you may never have "visited" before. Sometimes there's also information about what life was like for the people who lived there.

A Closer Look

Sometimes the best way to understand a text of Scripture is to compare the text to a related passage and/or its connected article. That's why you'll find symbols that "advertise" companion passages and articles that provide insight into the passage indicated.

Quote Unquote

Occasionally you might be interested in knowing what someone else besides the writers of Scripture had to say about an idea raised in the biblical text, or about the text itself. That's not to suggest that these quotations from various authors are on a par with Scripture. But one way to gain perspective on the implications of a passage is to read what someone has written, and then use that to reflect on what God has said.

THEMES TO CONSIDER

In designing The Word In Life Study Bible, *the editors wanted to create a resource that would help people deal with the issues of today, not yesterday. To that end, they identified a number of themes to highlight. Articles and other information provide a starting point for thought, study, and discussion of the following important areas:*

WORK

For most of us, work is the most dominating area of life. It determines where we'll live, what kind of lifestyle we'll have, even who our friends will be. Yet how many of us are aware of how much the Bible says about work and workplace issues?

ECONOMICS

Who can doubt the importance of economic issues in a world increasingly tied together in a giant global marketplace? Of course, Scripture wasn't written to be an economics textbook. Nevertheless, it gives us principles relating to

wealth, money, value, service, the environment, and other topics affecting both public policy and personal financial decisions.

ETHICS

This is the issue of right and wrong, of integrity and character. In a day when truth and values have become relative, we need to return to God's unchanging Word as our absolute standard for ethical conduct and commitments.

ETHNICITY

One has only to glance at a map of our modern world to recognize the impact of racial and ethnic differences. The landscape is strewn with wars, conflicts, and problems tied to long-standing ethnic tensions. How should Christians respond, especially living in an increasingly pluralistic society? As the early church discovered, the gospel has enormous implications for how we relate to others from different backgrounds.

THE CHURCH

Enormous opportunities and critical choices face the church today. A fresh look at the church's beginnings and its impact on the first-century world can offer valuable guidelines for the church's impact on the twenty-first-century world.

LAITY

Elton Trueblood has pointed out that the first Reformation put the Word of God back into the hands of the people of God; now we face the prospect of a "second reformation" that can put the *work* of God back into the hands of the people of God. This means that "everyday" believers can participate in carrying out God's work and find meaning and value in their efforts.

THE FAMILY

Building marriages and families that honor God has perhaps never been harder than today. That's why *The Word In Life Study Bible* highlights passages, principles, and people that show us the fundamental truths—and the honest realities—of building healthy family relationships in a fallen world.

THE CITY

Today for the first time in history, more people live in metropolitan than in rural areas. That has enormous implications for how Christians engage the world. Yet many believers have adopted a negative view of the city; some even see it as an evil. But when we read the Bible, we discover that the gospel "conquered" the Roman world by penetrating its major cities. The same thing can happen today.

WITNESS

One thing is certain about evangelism: both non-Christians and Christians feel uncomfortable with it. Yet Jesus has sent His followers into the world to communicate His message of salvation. Fortunately, the Bible gives us guidelines for carrying out the task in a way that is winsome, sensitive, and effective.

WOMEN

One of the most significant developments in recent culture has been the growing awareness of and sensitivity to issues and concerns of women—their dignity, their needs, and their rights. *The Word In Life Study Bible* places a special emphasis on the many women of the Scriptures and their significant contribution to the ministry of Jesus and the growth of the church. It also highlights the condition of women in the ancient world and the biblical teaching that pertains to the lives of women both then and now.

The themes mentioned above are just some of the ones that are touched on. It wouldn't be possible to classify them all. But as you use The Word In Life Study Bible, *it will stir up your thinking and show you other areas in which to apply God's Word to life.* ◆

HOW TO USE THE SYMBOL SYSTEM

The section above concerning 'Features to Look For' mentions four symbols that are used to designate various kinds of articles, tables, or related material in The Word In Life Study Bible.

From time to time as you read the biblical text, you will see one of those four symbols along the left side of the text, accompanied by a box containing information that will lead you to a feature that has to do with the biblical passage you are reading.

If the feature you are being sent to is on one of the two pages you are opened to (called a 'spread'), then the box next to the symbol by the text will

contain just chapter-and-verse information, designating one verse (for example, 1:10) or a range of verses (1:1–16). No page number is given. Just look on the spread you are opened to for a matching symbol accompanied by a box

containing the name of the symbol (such as CONSIDER THIS) and matching chapter-and-verse information.

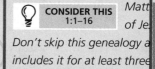

If the feature you are being sent to is someplace other than the spread you are opened to, then the box next to the symbol by the text will contain chapter-and-verse information and a page number. Just look on the designated

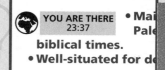

page for a matching symbol accompanied by a box containing the name of the symbol and matching chapter-and-verse information.

NEW KING JAMES FOOTNOTES

> your brethren*ᵃ* only, what do you do more *than* not even the tax collectors*ᵇ* do so? ⁴⁸Therefore

As you read, you will often see a raised letter in the biblical text. Each raised letter designates a New King James footnote, to be found at the foot of the text. Each footnote is designated by the chapter and verse in which its raised letter is contained. Then you will see the raised letter, followed by the footnote. (The letter *a* is used for the first footnote connected to each verse. If a verse has more than one footnote connected to it, then the second footnote receives the letter *b*. The chapter and verse are not repeated in such cases.)

New King James footnotes contain helpful information about significant textual variations and alternate translations, as well as some explanations and references to other passages of Scripture.

Footnotes concerning textual variations make no evaluation of readings, but do clearly indicate the manuscript sources of readings. They objectively present the facts without such remarks as 'the best manuscripts omit' or 'the most reliable manuscripts read,' which are value judgments that differ according to varying viewpoints on the text.

Where significant variations occur in the New Testament Greek manuscripts, textual notes are classified as followed:

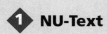 **NU-Text**

These variations from the traditional text represent the text as published in the twenty-sixth edition of the Nestle-Aland Greek New Testament (N) and in the United Bible Societies' third edition (U), hence the abbreviation, 'NU-Text.'

Example:

> As we forgive our debtors.
>
> *6:4 ᵃNU-Text omits openly.   6:6 ᵃNU-Text omits openly.*

 M-Text

These variations from the traditional text represent the Majority Text, which is based on the majority of surviving manuscripts. It should be noted that M stands for whatever reading is printed in the first edition of *The Greek New Testament According to the Majority Text,* whether supported by overwhelming, strong, or only a divided majority textual tradition.

Example:

> be baptized by him. ¹⁴And John *tried to* prevent
>
> *3:11 ᵃM-Text omits and fire.*

The textual notes reflect the scholarship of the past 150 years and will assist the reader to observe the variations between the different manuscript traditions of the New Testament. Such information is generally not available in English translations of the New Testament.

◆ ◆ ◆ ◆ ◆ ◆ ◆ ◆ ◆ ◆ ◆ ◆ ◆ ◆ ◆ ◆ ◆ ◆ ◆ ◆

OTHER FEATURES

MAPS

Many maps appear throughout The Word In Life Study Bible. They are designed to provide relevant geographical information in an accessible and easy-to-read format, on the same pages with the biblical text and related features.

A number of locator maps show you quickly where a certain place is with regard to its surrounding area.

CHORAZIN
A city condemned by Christ for not repenting.

Sidon
Mediterranean Sea
Capernaum • Bethsaida
GALILEE
Sea of Galilee
Nazareth •
Caesarea •
SAMARIA
DECAPOLIS
Jordan River
Joppa •

TABLES

Information is often presented in the form of tables or lists, showing at a glance how various facts and ideas relate to each other.

THE TWELVE	
Apostle	**Description**
Simon (Peter) (Mark 1:16)	Fisherman from Galilee, Andrew's brother
Andrew (John 1:40)	Fisherman from Galilee, Peter's brother
James	Son of Zebedee, brother to John; from Capernaum
John (Introduction to John)	Son of Zebedee, brother to James; from Capernaum
Philip	From Bethsaida
Bartholomew	From Cana in Galilee

A Gospel for the Thinking Person

The first-century world was a swirl of ideas, values, and symbols, not unlike our own. John's is a Gospel that is especially good for the thinking person. Unlike Matthew, Mark, and Luke, which present comprehensive and similar ("synoptic") overviews of the Lord's life, John is a highly stylized arrangement of carefully selected events and words, all directed toward one major purpose: that readers might find life by believing in Jesus as the Christ. John's goal is not belief for its own sake, but belief in order to have *life* (John 20:30–31).

For that reason, this book is vitally important for modern-day Christians. We tend to apply our faith only to certain private and "religious" settings, but leave it behind when we go into the public arena. The message of John cuts through that way of thinking and living. Jesus is our bridge between that which is eternal, spiritual, and supernatural, and the everyday, human, natural world. He is the divine Word of God, yet He became human and lived our experience (1:1, 14).

How can our faith become relevant to the day-to-day circumstances we face? In the Gospel of John, Jesus shows us. He lived the message that He preached. And as we come to know Him and follow Him, we can experience the *life* that He gives.

John

Christ is the divine Word of God, yet He became human.

· · · · · · · · · · · ·

CONTENTS

Under Authority (12:49)

Jesus modeled for us two principles of leading and following.

The Cost of Following Jesus (15:18–25)

Sooner or later, following Christ has a cost, and those who think they can get by without paying it are misguided. In fact, if there's no cost, is there really any genuine commitment?

Whose Job Is Evangelism? (16:8)

John shows that bringing people to faith is a cooperative effort between Christians and the Holy Spirit.

The Women around Jesus (19:25)

Women played a major part in Jesus' life and work. This listing summarizes their participation.

◆ ◆ ◆ ◆ ◆ ◆ ◆ ◆ ◆ ◆ ◆ ◆ ◆ ◆ ◆ ◆ ◆ ◆ ◆ ◆

THE SEVEN SIGNS OF JOHN'S GOSPEL

A famous author once said that the key to good writing is not in knowing what to put into a story, but what to leave out. Imagine, then, the problem of writing down the story of Jesus, especially if you had been an eyewitness and even a participant in the events. Of all that Jesus said and did, what would you include? What would you leave out?

John solved the problem by determining what he wanted his Gospel to accomplish: he wanted his readers to know that "Jesus is the Christ, the Son of God, and that believing [they might] have life in His name" (John 20:31). To that end, he organized his account around seven miracles that Jesus performed, seven "signs" pointing to His divine nature:

The fact that there are seven sign miracles is significant. In the Jewish view of life, the number seven signified perfection or completion. John's Gospel presents the seven miracles like a diamond refracting seven bands of color. Upon closer inspection, each one turns out to be rooted in Old Testament understanding of the Messiah. John's point is that Jesus is perfect and complete. His miracles show His true colors—that He is the Messiah that Israel has been looking for, and that He alone offers eternal life.

This way of presenting things may seem strange to some modern readers. But the Gospel of John, though probably the last Gospel to be written, was Christianity's first statement of the message of Jesus in a way that would relate to the thought-forms of its day. It is more meticulously and artistically composed than any prize-winning narrative or award-winning film. ◆

THE SIGNS AND THEIR MEANINGS	
Turns water into wine (2:1–12)	Jesus is the source of life.
Heals a nobleman's son (4:46–54)	Jesus is master over distance.
Heals a lame man at the pool of Bethesda (5:1–17)	Jesus is master over time.
Feeds 5,000 (6:1–14)	Jesus is the bread of life.
Walks on water, stills a storm (6:15–21)	Jesus is master over nature.
Heals a man blind from birth (9:1–41)	Jesus is the light of the world.
Raises Lazarus from the dead (11:17–45)	Jesus has power over death.

JOHN—THE APOSTLE OF LOVE

John and his brother James came from the prosperous family of Zebedee, a successful fisherman who owned his own boat and had hired servants (Mark 1:19–20). Together with Simon and Andrew, with whom they were in partnership (Luke 5:10), the brothers became loyal followers of Jesus. Their mother Salome also joined the fellowship and supported Jesus' ministry (Mark 15:4–41; Luke 8:3).

Modern Christians regard John as the "apostle of love" because of the frequent appearance of that theme in his writings and because the Gospel of John refers to him as the disciple whom Jesus loved (John 13:23). But he certainly didn't start out as a model of charity.

Apparently headstrong and opinionated, Jesus dubbed John and his brother the Sons of Thunder (Mark 3:17). On one occasion they created a storm of protest and indignation from the other disciples by asking if they could sit on Jesus' right and left hands in glory (Mark 10:35–45). On another occasion they suggested calling down fire from heaven on an unreceptive Samaritan village; Jesus rebuked them (Luke 9:51–56).

Somehow John's exposure to Jesus worked an amazing change in his life. After the Lord's departure, he became a leader of the Christian movement, as might be expected. But now his perspective was different. When word came that the gospel had spread to the Samaritans, John was sent with Peter to investigate. Whereas before he had wanted to destroy Samaritans, now he helped bring them the Holy Spirit (Acts

---

PERSONALITY PROFILE: JOHN

Name means: "Yahweh is gracious."

Home: Probably raised in Capernaum on the north shore of the Sea of Galilee; later lived at Ephesus; banished to the island of Patmos in old age.

Family: Father was Zebedee; mother was probably Salome; younger brother of James. Salome and Mary may have been sisters (Matt. 27:56; John 19:25); if so, James and John would have been cousins to Jesus.

Occupation: Commercial fisherman; later, one of Jesus' disciples and a member of His inner circle; also an author of a Gospel, three New Testament letters, and Revelation.

Best known today for: His close relationship to Jesus, and his New Testament writings.

8:14–25). The son of thunder had become a son of love!

Church tradition holds that after the execution of his brother James, John eventually migrated to Ephesus, from which he wrote or oversaw the writing of five New Testament documents. From there he was banished to the island of Patmos, but later returned to Ephesus where he died sometime after A.D. 98. ◆

CHAPTER 1

The Word

¹In the beginning was the Word, and the Word was with God, and the Word was God. ²He was in the beginning

🔅 **1:3**

with God. ³All things were made through Him, and without Him nothing was made that was made. ⁴In Him was life, and the life was the light of men. ⁵And the light shines in the darkness, and the darkness did not comprehend*ᵃ* it.

⁶There was a man sent from God, whose name *was* John. ⁷This man came for a witness, to bear witness of the Light, that all through him might believe. ⁸He was not that Light, but *was sent* to bear witness of that Light. ⁹That was the true Light which gives light to every man coming into the world.*ᵃ*

¹⁰He was in the world, and the world was made through Him, and the world did not know Him. ¹¹He came to His own,*ᵃ* and His own*ᵇ* did not receive Him. ¹²But as many as received Him, to them He gave the right to become children of God, to those who believe in His name: ¹³who were born, not of blood, nor of the will of the flesh, nor of the will of man, but of God.

🔅 **1:14**
see pg. 326

¹⁴And the Word became flesh and dwelt among us, and we beheld His glory, the glory as of the only begotten of the Father, full of grace and truth.

¹⁵John bore witness of Him and cried out, saying, "This was He of whom I said, 'He who comes after me is preferred before me, for He was before me.' "

¹⁶And*ᵃ* of His fullness we have all received, and grace for grace. ¹⁷For the law was given through Moses, *but* grace and truth came through Jesus Christ. ¹⁸No one has seen God at any time. The only begotten Son,*ᵃ* who is in the bosom of the Father, He has declared *Him.*

The Testimony of John the Baptist

¹⁹Now this is the testimony of John, when the Jews sent priests and Levites from Jerusalem to ask him, "Who are you?"

²⁰He confessed, and did not deny, but confessed, "I am not the Christ."

²¹And they asked him, "What then? Are you Elijah?"

He said, "I am not."

"Are you the Prophet?"

And he answered, "No."

1:5 ᵃOr *overcome*   1:9 ᵃOr *That was the true Light which, coming into the world, gives light to every man.*   1:11 ᵃThat is, *His own things or domain*   ᵇThat is, *His own people*
1:16 ᵃNU-Text reads *For.*   1:18 ᵃNU-Text reads *only begotten God.*

THE DIVINE PARTNERSHIP

🔅 **CONSIDER THIS**
1:3
Christ was fully involved in the work of creation (v. 3). In fact, all three persons of the Trinity worked together to bring the world into existence—Father (Gen. 1:1; John 5:17), Son (John 1:10; Col. 1:16), and Holy Spirit (Gen. 1:2; Job 33:4).

Many people tend to think of God's divine partnership only in terms of the work of salvation. But the three members of the Godhead are just as involved in the ongoing work of providing and caring for all creatures and maintaining the created order. In fact, their creative work continues even now in the heavens, as God prepares eternal dwelling places for believers (John 14:2–3; Rev. 21:1–2, 5).

Remarkably, this working, Triune God invites people to work with Him as junior members in the partnership, to accomplish His work in the world. In our day-to-day jobs, God asks us to do only what He has been doing from the beginning.

Perhaps you've never thought of God as a worker, but that's how He first appears in Scripture. See "God—The Original Worker," John 5:17.

Your own work is an extension of God's work in the world. See "People at Work," Heb. 2:7.

GOD AMONG US

 CONSIDER THIS
1:14

The first four-teen verses of John 1 were probably a hymn for the early church. They remind us that Jesus is God's Word (v. 1), "word" being a Greek term that means a thought expressed. Jesus is the human expression of God. He is light and flesh, to use John's metaphors (vv. 4–5, 14). To see Jesus is to see God, and to know Jesus is to experience God's grace and truth.

It is no accident, then, that believers are called to practice community and witness publicly. The gospel is both what we say and how we live. Just as Christ became flesh and "dwelt among us," so we are to "flesh out" the good news about Christ in our everyday world.

22Then they said to him, "Who are you, that we may give an answer to those who sent us? What do you say about yourself?"

23He said: "I *am*

'The voice of one crying in the wilderness:
"Make straight the way of the LORD," '*a*

as the prophet Isaiah said."

1:23 *a*Isaiah 40:3

* * * * * * * *

PERSONALITY PROFILE: ANDREW

 FOR YOUR INFO
1:40

Name means: "Manly."

Home: Bethsaida and Capernaum, on the northwest coast of the Sea of Galilee.

Family: Father's name was Jonah; brother was Simon Peter (see Mark 1:16).

Occupation: Fisherman; later one of Jesus' followers and, according to tradition, an apostle to Scythia (now Russia).

Known today as: The person who introduced Simon to the Lord.

ANDREW THE NETWORKER

In addition to working in his family's commercial fishing enterprise, Andrew followed the teaching of John the Baptist and was considered one of his disciples (John 1:35–40). Thus he heard John declare that Jesus was the Lamb of God—a clear reference to Him as the Messiah. Eager to know more about this new Teacher, Andrew pursued Jesus, prompting an invitation to spend an evening with Him. The meeting convinced Andrew that he had indeed met the long-awaited Christ.

The text is quite clear that the first thing Andrew did after coming to this conclusion was to find his brother, Simon, and tell him the extraordinary news: "We have found the Messiah!" He then brought his brother to meet Jesus (vv. 41–42).

Later, after Jesus called both of the brothers to follow Him as His disciples, Andrew and the others found themselves on one occasion confronted by thousands of people. Jesus asked His disciples where they could buy food for the crowd to eat, a proposition that staggered them.

²⁴Now those who were sent were from the Pharisees. ²⁵And they asked him, saying, "Why then do you baptize if you are not the Christ, nor Elijah, nor the Prophet?"

²⁶John answered them, saying, "I baptize with water, but there stands One among you whom you do not know. ²⁷It is He who, coming after me, is preferred before me, whose sandal strap I am not worthy to loose."

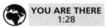 ²⁸These things were done in Bethabara[a] beyond the Jordan, where John was baptizing.

²⁹The next day John saw Jesus coming toward him, and said, "Behold! The Lamb of God who takes away the sin of the world! ³⁰This is He of whom I said, 'After me comes a Man who is preferred before me, for He was before me.' ³¹I did not know Him; but that He should be revealed to Israel, therefore I came baptizing with water."

³²And John bore witness, saying, "I saw the Spirit descending from heaven like a dove, and He remained upon Him. ³³I did not know Him, but He who sent me to baptize with water said to me, 'Upon whom you see the Spirit descending, and remaining on Him, this is He who baptizes with the Holy Spirit.' ³⁴And I have seen and testified that this is the Son of God."

1:28 ᵃNU-Text and M-Text read *Bethany*.

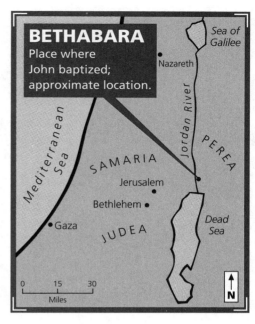

BETHABARA
Place where
John baptized;
approximate location.

BETHABARA

YOU ARE THERE
1:28
- A ford or crossing on the Jordan River at which John the Baptist carried out his work. The exact location is unknown.
- Name means "house of the ford," though it may also be another name for Bethany.

But Andrew had made the acquaintance of a boy with a handful of barley loaves and a couple of fish. He brought this meager supply to the attention of the Lord, who then multiplied it to feed the entire crowd of about 5,000 (6:4–14).

Shortly before Jesus' arrest, certain Greeks desired to meet Him. Once again, Andrew acted as a go-between, carrying their request to his Teacher (12:20–22). All of these incidents suggest that Andrew was a networker, a man who liked to put people together—and especially to put them together with Jesus. He serves as a model for believers today in bringing others to Christ.

Tradition holds that Andrew devoted the later years of his life to spreading the news about Jesus to Scythia, the region north of the Black Sea. Some say that he was martyred at Patrae in Achaia by crucifixion on an X-shaped cross. ◆

John 1

Jesus Recruits His First Followers

³⁵Again, the next day, John stood with two of his disciples. ³⁶And looking at Jesus as He walked, he said, "Behold the Lamb of God!"

³⁷The two disciples heard him speak, and they followed Jesus. ³⁸Then Jesus turned, and seeing them following, said to them, "What do you seek?"

They said to Him, "Rabbi" (which is to say, when translated, Teacher), "where are You staying?"

³⁹He said to them, "Come and see." They came and saw where He was staying, and remained with Him that day (now it was about the tenth hour).

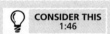 **1:40**
see pg. 326

⁴⁰One of the two who heard John speak, and followed Him, was Andrew, Simon Peter's brother. ⁴¹He first found his own brother Simon, and said to him, "We have found the Messiah" (which is translated, the Christ). ⁴²And he brought him to Jesus.

Now when Jesus looked at him, He said, "You are Simon the son of Jonah.ᵃ You shall be called Cephas" (which is translated, A Stone).

⁴³The following day Jesus wanted to go to Galilee, and He found Philip and said to him, "Follow Me." ⁴⁴Now Philip

1:45

was from Bethsaida, the city of Andrew and Peter. ⁴⁵Philip found Nathanael and said to him, "We have found Him of whom Moses in the

1:42 ᵃNU-Text reads John.

CONSIDER THIS
1:46

NAZARETH— THE OTHER SIDE OF THE TRACKS

Nazareth was a community on "the other side of the tracks." Located less than five miles from Sepphoris, the splendid capital city of Galilee, it knew quite well the impact on Palestine of Greek culture and Roman wealth and power. Yet Nazareth shared in none of those benefits. Its situation on a steep promontory ensured that its citizens would remain outsiders in the city below.

Someone has said that "God made the garden, evil men made the city, but the devil made the small town." Little towns can be vicious with rumors, gossip, and memories that refuse to die. They can also prove remarkably resistant to change. Nazareth in Jesus' day was possibly that kind of town.

Nevertheless, God chose Nazareth as the place where Jesus would grow up and invest most of His life. That fact demonstrates that while God cares deeply about cities, He also invests in small communities and various kinds of neighborhoods. Nazareth is a gift to anyone who comes from an unfashionable place, such as a dying inner city or

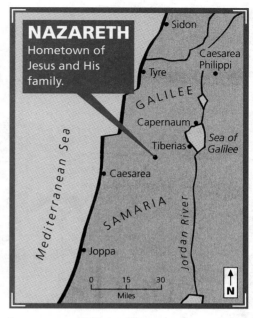

law, and also the prophets, wrote—Jesus of Nazareth, the son of Joseph."

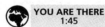
1:46 ⁴⁶And Nathanael said to him, "Can anything good come out of Nazareth?" Philip said to him, "Come and see."

⁴⁷Jesus saw Nathanael coming toward Him, and said of him, "Behold, an Israelite indeed, in whom is no deceit!"

⁴⁸Nathanael said to Him, "How do You know me?"

Jesus answered and said to him, "Before Philip called you, when you were under the fig tree, I saw you."

⁴⁹Nathanael answered and said to Him, "Rabbi, You are the Son of God! You are the King of Israel!"

⁵⁰Jesus answered and said to him, "Because I said to you, 'I saw you under the fig tree,' do you believe? You will see

1:51
see pg. 330 greater things than these." ⁵¹And He said to him, "Most assuredly, I say to you, hereafter[a] you shall see heaven open, and the angels of God ascending and descending upon the Son of Man."

CHAPTER 2

A Marriage Feast at Cana

2:1
see pg. 331 ¹On the third day there was a wedding in Cana of Galilee, and the mother of Jesus was there. ²Now both Jesus and His disciples were

(Bible text continued on page 331)

1:51 [a]NU-Text omits *hereafter*.

◆　◆　◆　◆　◆　◆　◆　◆　◆　◆　◆　◆

a declining rural town. Nazareth says that such a person, too, can receive God's love and serve the world.

If they want to, that is. Nazareth chose to reject its home-grown leader in dramatic fashion (Luke 4:16–30). Jesus left and as far as we know, never went back. However, His mother and brothers remained. They had to endure the scorn of their neighbors, who may have circulated rumors about Jesus' birth and His mental condition. The family might have suspected that Jesus' career would end in a martyr's death. For a while, even His brothers doubted His claims (John 7:5).

Can anything good come out of a Nazareth? Or out of a seedy neighborhood? Or out of an abandoned, forgotten piece of real estate? In Jesus, we see the answer is yes! ◆

Galilee, the province in which Nazareth was located, was a seedbed for revolutionaries against Rome. See "Galilee," Mark 1:14.

NAZARETH

YOU ARE THERE
1:45
• Name meant "watchtower"; also "shoot" or "sprout."

• Close enough to the main trade routes to maintain contact with the outside world, but its remote location contributed to a certain aloofness and independence. Its people, for example, spoke a crude dialect of Aramaic.

• Not highly regarded, as reflected in Nathanael's remark, "Can anything good come out of Nazareth?" (John 1:46).

• Hometown of Joseph and Mary and boyhood home of Jesus.

• Today, Nazareth is a mostly Arab village of about 65,000 to 70,000 residents. Tours frequent the Church of the Carpenter and a house in which Jesus allegedly grew up.

• Recent archaeological digs have uncovered sites for numerous Roman garrisons and cities within five miles of Nazareth.

SACRED SPACE

I n His conversation with Nathanael, Jesus alluded to the Old Testament incident we call Jacob's ladder (v. 51; Gen. 28:12). Jacob had a dream in which angels passed to and from heaven, where God stood and repeated promises He had made to Jacob's father and grandfather. Waking up, Jacob exclaimed, "Surely, the Lord is in this place."

By reminding Nathanael of that story, Jesus tapped into one of the most powerful concepts of Old Testament theology—the idea that a specific place on earth is made special because of God's presence there. To the Hebrews, wherever God or His representatives touched the ground, that spot became "Bethel," or sacred space (literally, "House of God"). They built altars in those places to commemorate God's visitation.

Jesus told Nathanael that someday angels would ascend and descend upon *Him.* That put a radically new twist on things: now there was not only sacred space, but a sacred

Person. Eventually, that truth came to have enormous implications, such as:

(1) *Those who have Christ become temples of God.* We as believers become sacred space, or better yet, sacred people because of God's presence within us. Paul described us as "temple[s] of the Holy Spirit" (1 Cor. 6:19).

(2) *Every place that we take Jesus becomes a special place.* God is in Christ and Christ is in us, so wherever we are—in the city, in the marketplace, at home—that place becomes sacred space because Christ is there, *in us.* As a result . . .

(3) *We can view our workplaces, neighborhoods, and communities from a new perspective.* We don't have to write them off as "secular" territory. And no longer are cathedrals and churches the only hallowed buildings in town. An office with Christians in it who expect God to work there becomes as special a place as any religious shrine. Even a fig tree can become the place where God carries out His purposes, as Nathanael discovered (John 1:50). Furthermore . . .

(4) *We need no longer view the inner city as throw-away real estate or a God-forsaken ghetto.* Any neighborhood, no matter how scarred and broken, can become a Bethel. If Christ's people are there, Christ is there. That sort of vision can transform a community and lend its

(continued on next page)

2:3
see pg. 332
invited to the wedding. ³And when they ran out of wine, the mother of Jesus said to Him, "They have no wine."

⁴Jesus said to her, "Woman, what does your concern have to do with Me? My hour has not yet come."

⁵His mother said to the servants, "Whatever He says to you, do it."

⁶Now there were set there six waterpots of stone, according to the manner of purification of the Jews, containing twenty or thirty gallons apiece. ⁷Jesus said to them, "Fill the waterpots with water." And they filled them up to the brim. ⁸And He said to them, "Draw some out now, and take it to the master of the feast." And they took it. ⁹When the master of the feast had tasted the water that was made wine, and

The Seven Signs of John's Gospel

WATER INTO WINE

CONSIDER THIS
2:1–12

Jesus' miracle of turning water into wine (vv. 1–12) was loaded with symbolism. Its placement at the beginning of John's Gospel is significant.

For Jews, wine represented life and abundance. No proper wedding would be without it. Wine symbolized the life of the party and the expectation of a good life to come for the newlyweds. But at Cana, just as the young couple prepared to launch a new life, the unthinkable happened—they ran out of wine. That may have been a common problem in that day, given that wedding festivities often lasted as long as a week. Nevertheless, it was discouraging and probably quite an embarrassment to the host. The party immediately began to wind down.

But Jesus seized the moment to reveal to His followers something of who He was. By producing wine from water, He astounded His disciples and encouraged their faith (v. 11).

However, the product was not merely wine, but the best wine (v. 10) In the same way, Jesus was the new wine bringing abundant life to Judaism, which, like the wedding, had run out of life and become spiritually empty.

(continued from previous page)

people significance and hope.

Jesus demonstrated the power of that new vision by going to the most sacred spot in Israel, the temple, and restoring it to its purpose of worship (2:13–22). Later He went to Samaria, to Mount Gerazim, the sacred place of the Samaritans (4:19–24), where He defined true worship. Then He went to a sacred pool in Jerusalem, Bethesda, where He healed a lame man (5:1–4). And so it goes throughout John's Gospel.

Sacred space is a vital concept for us who need a God as big as the city and as powerful as today's workplace. We carry with us the very Lord of the universe. He can make every place that we enter a place of grace and truth for us and for others. ◆

CANA

YOU ARE THERE
2:1

• A town near Nazareth, exact location unknown, though possibly at modern Kirf Kenna, four miles north of Nazareth, or perhaps the ruined city of Khirbet Kana, nine miles north of Nazareth.

• Name meant "place of reeds"; at Kirf Kenna, water springs and shady fig trees are still found.

• Mentioned in Scripture only by John, as the site of Jesus' first recorded miracle (John 2:1–11; 4:46) and the home of Nathanael (21:2).

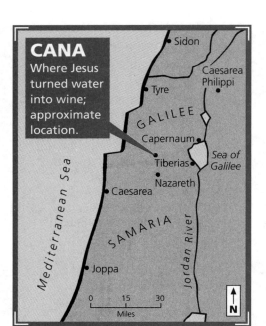

CANA
Where Jesus turned water into wine; approximate location.

did not know where it came from (but the servants who had drawn the water knew), the master of the feast called the bridegroom. [10]And he said to him, "Every man at the beginning sets out the good wine, and when the *guests* have well drunk, then the inferior. You have kept the good wine until now!"

2:1–12
see pg. 331

[11]This beginning of signs Jesus did in Cana of Galilee, and manifested His glory; and His disciples believed in Him.

2:12

[12]After this He went down to Capernaum, He, His mother, His brothers, and His disciples; and they did not stay there many days.

Merchants Evicted from the Temple

[13]Now the Passover of the Jews was at hand, and Jesus went up to Jerusalem. [14]And He found in the temple those who sold oxen and sheep and doves, and the money chang-

2:13–25

ers doing business. [15]When He had made a whip of cords, He drove them all out of the temple, with the sheep and the oxen, and poured out the changers' money and overturned the tables. [16]And He said to those who sold doves, "Take these things away! Do not make My Father's house a house of merchandise!"

• •

Good and Angry

 A CLOSER LOOK
2:13–25

What injustices cause your blood to boil? Jesus showed how to be both compassionate and angry in appropriate ways (vv. 13–25). See "Compassion and Anger in One Person?" Luke 19:41–46.

WINEMAKING

 YOU ARE THERE
2:3

Wine was a common beverage throughout biblical times. Galilee in particular was known for its cultivation of grapes and knowledge of the winemaking process.

Galilean women and children pressed grapes in a winepress dug out of limestone. Often an artificial cave constructed near the work area served as a wine cellar.

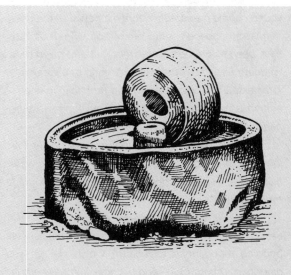

¹⁷Then His disciples remembered that it was written, "Zeal for Your house has eaten*a* Me up."*b*

¹⁸So the Jews answered and said to Him, "What sign do You show to us, since You do these things?"

 2:19–20 ¹⁹Jesus answered and said to them, "Destroy this temple, and in three days I will raise it up."

²⁰Then the Jews said, "It has taken forty-six years to build this temple, and will You raise it up in three days?"

²¹But He was speaking of the temple of His body. ²²Therefore, when He had risen from the dead, His disciples remembered that He had said this to them;*a* and they believed the Scripture and the word which Jesus had said.

²³Now when He was in Jerusalem at the Passover, during the feast, many believed in His name when they saw the signs which He did. ²⁴But Jesus did not commit Himself to them, because He knew all *men,* ²⁵and had no need that anyone should testify of man, for He knew what was in man.

CHAPTER 3

Nicodemus Visits Jesus by Night

¹There was a man of the Pharisees named Nicodemus, a ruler of the Jews. ²This man came to Jesus by night and said to Him, "Rabbi, we know that You are a teacher come from God; for no one can do these signs that You do unless God is with him."

³Jesus answered and said to him, "Most assuredly, I say to you, unless one is born again, he cannot see the kingdom of God."

⁴Nicodemus said to Him, "How can a man be born when he is old? Can he enter a second time into his mother's womb and be born?"

⁵Jesus answered, "Most assuredly, I say to you, unless one is born of water and the Spirit, he cannot enter the kingdom of God. ⁶That which is born of the flesh is flesh, and that which is born of the Spirit is spirit. ⁷Do not marvel that I said to you, 'You must be born again.' ⁸The wind blows where it wishes, and you hear the sound of it, but cannot tell where it comes from and where it goes. So is everyone who is born of the Spirit."

⁹Nicodemus answered and said to Him, "How can these things be?"

¹⁰Jesus answered and said to him, "Are you the teacher of Israel, and do not know these things? ¹¹Most assuredly, I say

(Bible text continued on page 335)

2:17 *a*NU-Text and M-Text read *will eat.* *b*Psalm 69:9 2:22 *a*NU-Text and M-Text omit *to them.*

WHAT HAPPENED TO MARY?

CONSIDER THIS 2:12 **Jesus' mother, brothers, and disciples accompanied Him during His early travels to Capernaum (v. 12). But after this scene, Jesus' mother disappears from John's account until Jesus' crucifixion (19:25–27). Was Mary a follower of her Son? Perhaps not in the sense of one who traveled with Him. It could be that over time she came to understand better her Son's divine nature and call. After His departure, she was found among those in the upper room who prayed and waited for the promise of the Holy Spirit (Acts 1:14).**

BUILDING THE TEMPLE

 YOU ARE THERE 2:19–20 **During Jesus' time, the temple at Jerusalem was undergoing extensive reconstruction and renovation. Desiring favor among the Jews, King Herod pledged to build a magnificent temple that would perhaps recall some of the glory of Solomon's temple (1 Kin. 6:1). Work began in 19 B.C. and was carried on until A.D. 64.**

At first the priests opposed Herod, suspicious that his real intent was to either do away with the temple altogether or erect something profane in its place. But Herod proved he was serious, hiring 10,000 laborers and ordering 1,000 wagons for hauling cream-colored stone. When finished, the structure shone so brightly in the Mediterranean sun that it was difficult to look at directly.

Still the priests feared that this most sacred place would be profaned.

(continued on next page)

(continued from previous page)

So Herod had 1,000 of them trained as carpenters and masons so that only priestly hands would construct the Most Holy Place. Unfortunately, the priests themselves turned out to be their own worst enemies: poor craftsmen, they did work that sometimes collapsed and had to be replaced.

But it was an exercise in futility. In A.D. 70, Roman armies surrounded Jerusalem, captured it, and completely destroyed Herod's temple (see "Jerusalem Surrounded," Luke 21:20).

The temple was but one of many splendid edifices that the family of the Herods built while they governed Palestine. Unfortunately, they are remembered more for their infamous family history than their brilliant architectural achievements. See "The Herods," Acts 12:1–2.

 CONSIDER THIS
3:21

THE GOSPEL IN A PLURALISTIC SOCIETY

Jesus' nighttime meeting with Nicodemus (vv. 1–21) and His midday encounter with the Samaritan woman (4:5–42) show two of the many different ways in which He dealt with people. Whether it had to do with a respected urban leader like Nicodemus or a hardened, street-wise loner like the woman of Samaria, Jesus approached people on their own terms, as individuals with unique concerns. He modeled for us what it means to live, work, and communicate the gospel message in a pluralistic society.

Nicodemus was an upper-class Jew, a Pharisee from one of the prominent families of Jerusalem. He approached Jesus, alone, at night. The Lord confronted him with his need to be "born again," then let him go away to think things over. The next time we see him, he is defending Jesus on a procedural matter (7:45–52). But Nicodemus apparently didn't openly identify with Jesus until after the crucifixion, when he helped prepare His body for burial (19:39).

The Samaritan woman, on the other hand, had lived a scandalous lifestyle with a succession of husbands and then with a live-in companion. As a result, her community despised her. She also probably came from mixed ancestry,

to you, We speak what We know and testify what We have seen, and you do not receive Our witness. ¹²If I have told you earthly things and you do not believe, how will you believe if I tell you heavenly things? ¹³No one has ascended to heaven but He who came down from heaven, *that is,* the Son of Man who is in heaven.*ᵃ* ¹⁴And as Moses lifted up the serpent in the wilderness, even so must the Son of Man be lifted up, ¹⁵that whoever believes in Him should not perish but*ᵃ* have eternal life. ¹⁶For God so loved the world that He gave His only begotten Son, that whoever believes in Him should not perish but have everlasting life. ¹⁷For God did not send His Son into the world to condemn the world, but that the world through Him might be saved.

¹⁸"He who believes in Him is not condemned; but he who does not believe is condemned already, because he has not believed in the name of the only begotten Son of God. ¹⁹And this is the condemnation, that the light has come into the world, and men loved darkness rather than light, because their deeds were evil. ²⁰For everyone practicing evil hates the light and does not come to the light, lest his deeds should be exposed. ²¹But he who does the truth comes to the light, that his

3:21

3:13 ᵃNU-Text omits *who is in heaven.*   3:15 ᵃNU-Text omits *not perish but.*

for which the Jews despised her. She was spoken to by Jesus in broad daylight, in public, first by herself but later in the company of others. He told her of "living water" and the need to worship in spirit and truth. She responded much more quickly than Nicodemus. Furthermore, hers may have been not so much an individual choice as a clan decision (4:39–41).

John went on to record many other ways Jesus dealt with people, and many ways they responded to Him. Some became believers after they were fed (6:4–14), others after they were healed (9:1–38), and others after they had seen the resurrected Christ (20:24–29). Some responded to the Lord's miracles, others to His teaching. There was no one kind of response to Jesus.

We as believers today must present the gospel in an increasingly pluralistic world. Like Jesus, we need to use many different approaches. What are some of the creative means you can use to influence friends and coworkers for Christ? ◆

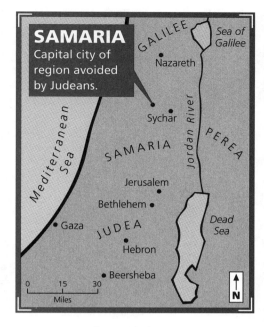

SAMARIA
Capital city of region avoided by Judeans.

SAMARIA

YOU ARE THERE 4:4 • **The central province of Palestine under the Romans. Its key city, also called Samaria, had been the capital of the northern kingdom of Israel before its fall to Assyria (722 B.C.).**
- **Noted for rich, fertile farmlands that produced valuable grain crops, olives, and grapes.**
- **Served by five major roads, which encouraged trade with Phoenicia, Syria, and Egypt.**
- **Historically, a prime target of invaders due to its reputation for prosperity.**

Jesus taught His followers a series of courses on relating to Samaritans. For two of the more memorable, see "Condemnation or Compassion?" Luke 9:51–56, and "Who Was the Neighbor?" Luke 10:37.

In going from Jerusalem to the end of the earth, the gospel had to go through Samaria. See "Opportunities Look Like Barriers," Acts 1:4.

deeds may be clearly seen, that they have been done in God."

John the Baptist Teaches about Jesus

²²After these things Jesus and His disciples came into the land of Judea, and there He remained with them and baptized. ²³Now John also was baptizing in Aenon near Salim, because there was much water there. And they came and were baptized. ²⁴For John had not yet been thrown into prison.

²⁵Then there arose a dispute between *some* of John's disciples and the Jews about purification. ²⁶And they came to John and said to him, "Rabbi, He who was with you beyond the Jordan, to whom you have testified—behold, He is baptizing, and all are coming to Him!"

²⁷John answered and said, "A man can receive nothing unless it has been given to him from heaven. ²⁸You yourselves bear me witness, that I said, 'I am not the Christ,' but, 'I have been sent before Him.' ²⁹He who has the bride is the bridegroom; but the friend of the bridegroom, who stands and hears him, rejoices greatly because of the bridegroom's voice. Therefore this joy of mine is fulfilled. **3:30** ³⁰He must increase, but I *must* decrease. ³¹He who comes from above is above all; he who is of the earth is earthly and speaks of the earth. He who comes from heaven is above all. ³²And what He has seen and heard, that He testifies; and no one receives His testimony. ³³He who has received His testimony has certified that God is true. ³⁴For He whom God has sent speaks the words of God, for God does not give the Spirit by measure. ³⁵The Father loves the Son, and has given all things into His hand. ³⁶He who believes in the Son has everlasting life; and he who does not believe the Son shall not see life, but the wrath of God abides on him."

CHAPTER 4

Jesus Encounters a Samaritan Woman

¹Therefore, when the Lord knew that the Pharisees had heard that Jesus made and baptized more disciples than John ²(though Jesus Himself did not baptize, but His disciples), ³He left Judea and departed again to Galilee. ⁴But He needed to go through Samaria.

4:4 see pg. 335

4:5 see pg. 339

⁵So He came to a city of Samaria which is called Sychar, near the plot of ground that Jacob gave to his son Joseph. ⁶Now Jacob's well was

> "**A** MAN CAN RECEIVE NOTHING UNLESS IT HAS BEEN GIVEN TO HIM FROM HEAVEN."
> —John 3:27

(Bible text continued on page 338)

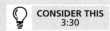
SUCCESS

To what extent should Christ's followers today pursue success? John's declaration that "He must increase, but I must decrease" (v. 30) seems to repudiate the idea of personal achievement, recognition, or material gain—common measures of success in our society. Indeed, John himself showed none of the outward trappings of a successful ministry (see "John the Street Preacher," Matt. 3:4).

So should believers avoid success as the world defines it? Can people be successful in their careers as well as in their spiritual lives, or are the two mutually exclusive? Some Christians say that success on the job creates credibility for them to talk about Christ with coworkers. Others, however, claim that they have no interest in being successful. But is that a genuine conviction, or are they merely avoiding the rough-and-tumble of a competitive marketplace? Would God prefer that His people be *failures* on the job, in society, or in life?

Questions like these barely scratch the surface of the complex, emotional issue of success. The people of Jesus' day were no less interested in prospering than we are, even if they defined success in slightly different terms. So it's not surprising that Scripture speaks to human ambition and achievement. It seems to affirm at least three important principles, as illustrated by John the Baptist:

(1) *Success is always measured by a set of standards established by some person or group.* Many people of John's day felt that they were assured of the blessing of God simply because they were descendants of Abraham. Their religious leaders aggressively promoted and reinforced that idea (Matt. 3:7–9; Luke 3:8; John 8:39). John challenged them to reconsider that way of thinking. What mattered, he said, was faith in Jesus. That was the ultimate criterion by which God would measure people's lives. Thus, unbelief would result in the ultimate failure— eternal death (3:36).

(2) *Why and how we pursue success is just as important as whether or not we achieve it.* John's listeners were ordinary people caught up in the everyday scramble to get ahead. But in their pursuit of gain they tended to ignore the needs of others and to take ethical shortcuts. John challenged them to make internal changes (that is, to repent) and to demonstrate those changes in their day-to-day responsibilities through charity, honesty, and justice (Luke 3:8, 10–14).

John himself was able to carry out his ministry because he had the right perspective on the assignment that God had given him. He recognized that he was merely a forerunner to the Christ, not the Christ Himself (John 3:28–29). He knew that Jesus' ministry was going to grow and expand, slowly eliminating the need for John—hence his statement that "He must increase, but I must decrease."

(3) *Obtaining success always carries a cost.* John warned the people of God's judgment using a simple, well-known image: "Even now the ax is laid to the root of the trees. Therefore, every tree which does not bear fruit is cut down and thrown into the fire" (Luke 3:9). Just as a lumberjack would lay his ax at the foot of a tree while he decided which trees in a forest to cut, so God had sent John and Jesus as His final messengers before letting His judgment fall.

The people could choose what they wanted to do— whether to continue in their self-satisfied ways of unbelief, or whether to turn toward God in repentance and obedience. Either way, there would be a cost involved. Unfortunately, most of them chose to reject John's message and later Jesus' message, with tragic results (see "Jerusalem Surrounded," Luke 21:20).

For John, the cost of faithfully proclaiming his message was imprisonment and, eventu-

(continued on next page)

(continued from previous page)

ally, execution (Matt. 14:1–12). Yet he gained a treasure all out of proportion to the price of martyrdom——the praise of Christ (11:7–11).

So should believers pursue success? Judging from the experience of John the Baptist and the people who followed him, the issue seems to be not so much *whether* we should pursue it, but *how*. In light of John's message, it's worth considering three crucial questions:

- Who sets the standards by which I measure success?
- What are my motives and behavior in pursuing success?
- What price am I willing to pay to achieve success? ◆

Jesus told a parable in which He showed that "True Success Means Faithfulness." See Matt. 25:14–30.

Like John, Paul challenged the idea of people looking out chiefly for Number One. See "Humility—The Scandalous Virtue," Phil. 2:3.

there. Jesus therefore, being wearied from *His* journey, sat thus by the well. It was about the sixth hour.

7A woman of Samaria came to draw water. Jesus said to her, "Give Me a drink." 8For His disciples had gone away into the city to buy food.

4:9 see pg. 340 9Then the woman of Samaria said to Him, "How is it that You, being a Jew, ask a drink from me, a Samaritan woman?" For Jews have no dealings with Samaritans.

10Jesus answered and said to her, "If you knew the gift of God, and who it is who says to you, 'Give Me a drink,' you would have asked Him, and He would have given you living water."

11The woman said to Him, "Sir, You have nothing to draw with, and the well is deep. Where then do You get that living water? 12Are You greater than our father Jacob, who gave us the well, and drank from it himself, as well as his sons and his livestock?"

13Jesus answered and said to her, "Whoever drinks of this water will thirst again, 14but whoever drinks of the water that I shall give him will never thirst. But the water that I shall give him will become in him a fountain of water springing up into everlasting life."

15The woman said to Him, "Sir, give me this water, that I may not thirst, nor come here to draw."

16Jesus said to her, "Go, call your husband, and come here."

17The woman answered and said, "I have no husband."

Jesus said to her, "You have well said, 'I have no husband,' 18for you have had five husbands, and the one whom you now have is not your husband; in that you spoke truly."

4:19–23 see pg. 341 19The woman said to Him, "Sir, I perceive that You are a prophet. 20Our fathers worshiped on this mountain, and you *Jews* say that in Jerusalem is the place where one ought to worship."

21Jesus said to her, "Woman, believe Me, the hour is coming when you will neither on this mountain, nor in Jerusalem, worship the Father. 22You worship what you do not know; we know what we worship, for salvation is of the Jews. 23But the hour is coming, and now is, when the true worshipers will worship the Father in spirit and truth; for the Father is seeking such to worship Him. 24God *is* Spirit, and those who worship Him must worship in spirit and truth."

25The woman said to Him, "I know that Messiah is coming" (who is called Christ). "When He comes, He will tell us all things."

26Jesus said to her, "I who speak to you am *He*."

4:27
see pg. 342
²⁷And at this *point* His disciples came, and they marveled that He talked with a woman; yet no one said, "What do You seek?" or, "Why are You talking with her?"

4:4–42
see pg. 342
²⁸The woman then left her waterpot, went her way into the city, and said to the men, ²⁹"Come, see a Man who told me all things that I ever did. Could this be the Christ?" ³⁰Then they went out of the city and came to Him.

³¹In the meantime His disciples urged Him, saying, "Rabbi, eat."

³²But He said to them, "I have food to eat of which you do not know."

³³Therefore the disciples said to one another, "Has anyone brought Him *anything* to eat?"

³⁴Jesus said to them, "My food is to do the will of Him who sent Me, and to finish His work. ³⁵Do you not say, 'There are still four months and *then* comes the harvest'? Behold, I say to you, lift up your eyes and look at the fields, for they are already white for harvest! ³⁶And he who reaps receives wages, and gathers fruit for eternal life, that both he who sows and he who reaps may rejoice together. ³⁷For in this the saying is true: 'One sows and another reaps.' ³⁸I sent you to reap that for which you have not labored; others have labored, and you have entered into their labors."

³⁹And many of the Samaritans of that city believed in Him because of the word of the woman who testified, "He told me all that I *ever* did." ⁴⁰So when the Samaritans had come to Him, they urged Him to stay with them; and He stayed there two days. ⁴¹And many more believed because of His own word.

⁴²Then they said to the woman, "Now we believe, not because of what you said, for we ourselves have heard *Him* and we know that this is indeed the Christ,ᵃ the Savior of the world."

Jesus Heals a Nobleman's Son

⁴³Now after the two days He departed from there and went to Galilee. ⁴⁴For Jesus Himself testified that a prophet has no honor in his own country. ⁴⁵So when He came to Galilee, the Galileans received Him, having seen all the things He did in Jerusalem at the feast; for they also had gone to the feast.

4:46–54
see pg. 343
⁴⁶So Jesus came again to Cana of Galilee where He had made the water wine. And there was a certain nobleman whose son was sick at Capernaum. ⁴⁷When he heard that Jesus had come out of Judea into Galilee, he went to Him and implored

4:42 ᵃNU-Text omits *the Christ.*

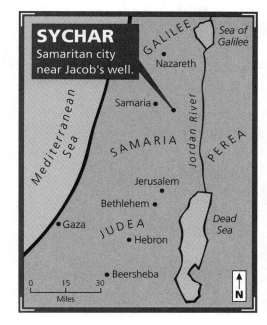

SYCHAR
Samaritan city near Jacob's well.

SYCHAR

YOU ARE THERE
4:5
- **A Samaritan city mentioned only once in the Bible (John 4:5).**
- **Exact location unknown, though it could be the same as ancient Askar, one mile north of Jacob's well, or possibly Shechem, a city of great historical significance (Gen. 33:18).**
- **Today some 300 Samaritan descendants live in Nablus, site of ancient Shechem.**

Him to come down and heal his son, for he was at the point

4:48 see pg. 344 of death. [48]Then Jesus said to him, "Unless you *people* see signs and wonders, you will by no means believe."

[49]The nobleman said to Him, "Sir, come down before my child dies!"

4:50 [50]Jesus said to him, "Go your way; your son lives." So the man believed the word that Jesus spoke to him, and he went his way. [51]And as he

• •

A Wealthy Man Believes

A CLOSER LOOK **4:50** *The nobleman who sought Jesus' help (v. 46) became a true child of God because he believed the words of Christ (v. 50). His status with God was based on his faith, not his wealth. Anyone whose greatest aspiration is status and wealth, rather than faith, has embarked on a course that can only end in eternal poverty. See "Christians and Money," 1 Tim. 6:7–19, and "Getting Yours," James 5:1–6. To find out about some of the other wealthy people in the New Testament, see Matt. 27:57.*

CONSIDER THIS
4:9

"JEWS HAVE NO DEALINGS WITH SAMARITANS"

Hatred between Jews and Samaritans was fierce and long-standing. In some ways, it dated all the way back to the days of the patriarchs. Jacob (or Israel) had twelve sons, whose descendants became twelve tribes. Joseph, his favorite, was despised by the other brothers (Gen. 37:3–4), and they attempted to do away with him.

But God intervened and not only preserved Joseph's life, but used him to preserve the lives of the entire clan. Before his death, Jacob gave Joseph a blessing in which he called him a "fruitful bough by a well" (Gen. 49:22). The blessing was fulfilled, as the territory allotted to the tribes of Joseph's two sons, Ephraim ("doubly fruitful") and Manasseh, was the fertile land that eventually became Samaria.

Later, Israel divided into two kingdoms. The northern kingdom, called Israel, established its capital first at Shechem, a revered site in Jewish history, and later at the hilltop city of Samaria.

In 722 B.C. Assyria conquered Israel and took most of its people into captivity. The invaders then brought in Gentile colonists "from Babylon, Cuthah, Ava, Hamath, and from Sepharvaim" (2 Kin. 17:24) to resettle the land. The foreigners brought with them their pagan idols, which the remaining Jews began to worship alongside the God of Israel (2 Kin. 17:29–41). Intermarriages also took place (Ezra 9:1—10:44; Neh. 13:23–28).

was now going down, his servants met him and told *him,* saying, "Your son lives!"

⁵²Then he inquired of them the hour when he got better. And they said to him, "Yesterday at the seventh hour the fever left him." ⁵³So the father knew that *it was* at the same hour in which Jesus said to him, "Your son lives." And he himself believed, and his whole household.

⁵⁴This again *is* the second sign Jesus did when He had come out of Judea into Galilee.

CHAPTER 5

Jesus Heals a Paralyzed Man

5:1–17
see pg. 343
¹After this there was a feast of the Jews, and Jesus went up to Jerusalem. ²Now there is in Jerusalem by the Sheep *Gate* a pool, which is

(Bible text continued on page 345)

❖ ❖ ❖ ❖ ❖ ❖ ❖ ❖ ❖ ❖ ❖ ❖ ❖ ❖ ❖ ❖ ❖ ❖

Meanwhile, the southern kingdom of Judah fell to Babylon in 600 B.C. Its people, too, were carried off into captivity. But 70 years later, a remnant of 43,000 was permitted to return and rebuild Jerusalem. The people who now inhabited the former northern kingdom—the Samaritans—vigorously opposed the repatriation and tried to undermine the attempt to reestablish the nation. For their part, the full-blooded, monotheistic Jews detested the mixed marriages and worship of their northern cousins. So walls of bitterness were erected on both sides and did nothing but harden for the next 550 years.

There are countless modern parallels to the Jewish-Samaritan enmity—indeed, wherever peoples are divided by racial and ethnic barriers. Perhaps that's why the Gospels and Acts provide so many instances of Samaritans coming into contact with the message of Jesus. It is not the person from the radically different culture on the other side of the world that is hardest to love, but the nearby neighbor whose skin color, language, rituals, values, ancestry, history, and customs are different from one's own.

Jews had no dealings with the Samaritans. With whom do you have no dealings? ◆

ETHNIC GAMES WITH RELIGIOUS ROOTS

CONSIDER THIS 4:19–23 **Jesus must have made the woman at the well very uncomfortable when He spoke with such detailed, personal knowledge of her past (v. 17). Perhaps that's why she began to play ethnic games with Him, falling back on her religious roots (vv. 19–20).**

Samaritans were good at that. Nearby was Mount Ebal, where Joshua had renewed Israel's covenant with God (Josh. 8:30–35). According to the Jewish Torah (Deut. 27:4–6), Mount Ebal was also where Moses built an altar to celebrate the Israelites entering the Promised Land. But the Samaritans held that Mount Gerizim, also nearby, was the only true place of worship. The Samaritans built an altar there in 400 B.C., but the Jews destroyed it in 128 B.C. That only added to the historic enmity between the two groups—and provided ammunition for the woman to challenge Jesus.

Today, many people still play ethnic games with their religious roots. In Mexico City, for example, some churches are located on top of Aztec or Mayan shrines. Some Mexicans, seeking to recover their Indian roots and throw off their Spanishness, literally dig deep into their past to promote paganism and reject Christianity. Similar behavior can be found among other groups exploring and recovering their roots. Like the Samaritans in Jesus' day, they want to affirm who they are as a people.

Jesus understood this woman's need for ethnic identity and security. But He challenged her and her neighbors with a deeper issue—their need to turn to God and become true worshipers of Him. He refused to play ethnic games when there was a matter of eternal life and death at stake.

JESUS SPEAKS TO A WOMAN

 CONSIDER THIS
4:27

The disciples marveled that their rabbi was speaking to a woman (v. 27). In their day it was considered disreputable and beneath his dignity for a rabbi to speak to a woman in public. But Jesus chose a more inclusive posture than His religious peers.

Women were not the only group that Jesus reached out to in contrast to other rabbis. See "Please Bless Our Children," Matt. 19:13–15.

 CONSIDER THIS
4:4–42

THE ROAD LESS TRAVELED

For Jews in Jesus' day, the main road to Jerusalem went around *Samaria*. But He intentionally went through *Samaria (v. 4)*, where He taught His disciples a lesson in cross-cultural communication.

Finding a woman at Jacob's well in Sychar (vv. 5–7), Jesus struck up a conversation which quickly turned personal. Before long, the woman was on the verge of conversion. But Jesus understood that in her culture women lacked authority to make substantive decisions on their own. Those were made by men, often tribally, within clans. In fact, it was unusual for a man, particularly a rabbi, to hold serious conversation with a woman in public, as Jesus was doing. Perhaps that's one reason why the woman left as soon as the disciples showed up (vv. 27–28).

However, another reason was so that she could go and tell her "significant others," her network of family and friends, about Jesus (vv. 28–30). The woman left her waterpot at the well, maybe because she was in a hurry, though she may have left it there to avoid having to carry it around; after all, she clearly intended to return. At any rate, v. 28 specifically points out that she approached "the men" in the community first—perhaps a clue that they were indeed the decision makers.

THE NOBLEMAN'S SON

 CONSIDER THIS
4:46–54 *The key to understanding the significance of Jesus' second sign miracle (vv. 46–54) is geography. The nobleman and his dying son lived in Capernaum, the main city of the Galilee region (see Luke 4:31). But Jesus was 20 miles away at Cana (where, significantly, His first sign miracle had taken place, John 2:1–12). That means that the nobleman walked a 40-mile round trip—a two-day trek by foot—to implore Jesus to heal his son. But Jesus merely spoke a word (v. 50), producing results 20 miles away, in a world that knew nothing of phones, faxes, or modems. No wonder the incident produced faith (v. 53). Jesus was the master of distance.*

But it was also true that she had been married to or had lived with or been intimate with a number of the men in that clan (vv. 17–18). In that respect, she was like many public aid mothers today living in common-law marriages. Those connections might have made her a unique "gatekeeper" or social organizer in the community. She could unlock the village for Jesus. Once she did, He stayed there for two days (v. 43).

What does Jesus' example say about communicating the gospel message today? Northern European and American cultures tend to value individual choice. But elsewhere, many cultures are more clannish. Inter- and intra-family relationships have a powerful bearing on how the message will be received. Western believers need to respect that and use it to advantage as they cross over into cultures different from their own.

Jesus followed the less-traveled road directly into Samaria to bring not just an individual woman, but an entire community to faith. Have you chosen the road less traveled to walk with Jesus into cultures different than your own? ◆

THE MAN AT BETHESDA

 CONSIDER THIS
5:1–17 *Jesus' third sign miracle revolves around the issue of time. The man at the pool of Bethesda had lain there for 38 years—an entire lifetime as a helpless cripple. Indeed, he had probably started lying there before Jesus was even born. Imagine the disappointment he must have experienced time after time when the angel stirred up the pool, but always he had arrived too late to experience healing. Yet Jesus healed him and immediately he was able to walk. Jesus showed Himself to be the master of time. However, was Israel ready for Him (v. 16)?*

MYTH: SCIENCE IS IN CONFLICT WITH CHRISTIAN FAITH

Many people today accept a number of myths about Christianity, with the result that they never respond to Jesus as He really is. This is one of ten articles that speak to some of those misconceptions. For a list of all ten, see 1 Tim. 1:3–4.

The people of Jesus' day demanded miraculous signs as a condition for belief (v. 48). Yet even though Jesus performed astonishing miracles, His Jewish brothers and sisters by and large rejected Him as their Messiah (1:11). Today many people reject Christianity on similar grounds. We live in a natural world, they say, a world that can be explained by science. Since Christianity relies on faith, it no longer applies in our modern, scientific world. In fact, Christianity and science conflict.

The interesting thing is that while many top scientists do not make this claim, many untrained people do. They have bought into a number of myths, including:

Science can be proved; Christianity cannot. The truth is that both science and Christianity deal with *evidence.* Science examines evidence about our world from things that we can see, touch, measure, and calculate. Christianity is based on evidence about our world from the life, teaching, death, and resurrection of Jesus. Both deal with matters that are very much open to examination.

Of course, it is a misconception that science can be "proved." The heart of the scientific method is to allow the evidence to lead one where it will.

But in that case, one cannot "prove" a scientific hypothesis, but only support it with evidence. In fact, one of the fundamental tenets of science is that it takes only one contrary instance to bring down an entire hypothesis. For centuries Newton's theories of gravity seemed irrefutably "proven." Then along came Einstein. Today his thinking is giving way to new discoveries.

Science is progressive; Christianity resists progress. There is some truth to this—but only some. At certain times in history, Christianity has opposed ideas that seemed to challenge its worldview. Yet at other times Christianity—that is to say, Christians—have been (and still are) on the vanguard of scientific progress. Indeed, modern science is largely the product of inquiring believers.

Science is logical; Christianity involves a leap of faith. Without question there is a logic and an order in scientific inquiry. But the same is true for the philosophical, historical, ethical, and theological disciplines of Christianity. Our faith is not opposed to reason. At points it may go beyond reason. But it is a reasonable faith. It hangs together logically.

At the same time, science demands an element of faith. Faith is not, as one schoolboy defined it, believing what you know is not true; faith involves self-commitment on the basis of evidence. In science, one must commit oneself to the belief that the world we see and touch is real, that nature is uniform, and that it operates according to the principle of cause-and-effect. Without these prior "leaps of faith," reasonable though they are, one cannot undertake science.

Science deals with the laws of nature; Christianity thrives on miracles. If science involves a closed, physical universe with fixed, unalterable laws, then the concept of miracles, which in-

(continued on next page)

called in Hebrew, Bethesda,[a] having five porches. [3]In these lay a great multitude of sick people, blind, lame, paralyzed, waiting for the moving of the water. [4]For an angel went down at a certain time into the pool and stirred up the water; then whoever stepped in first, after the stirring of the water, was made well of whatever disease he had.[a] [5]Now a certain man was there who had an infirmity thirty-eight years. [6]When Jesus saw him lying there, and knew that he already had been *in that condition* a long time, He said to him, "Do you want to be made well?"

[7]The sick man answered Him, "Sir, I have no man to put me into the pool when the water is stirred up; but while I am coming, another steps down before me."

5:8–18 [8]Jesus said to him, "Rise, take up your bed and walk." [9]And immediately the man was made well, took up his bed, and walked.

And that day was the Sabbath. [10]The Jews therefore said to him who was cured, "It is the Sabbath; it is not lawful for you to carry your bed."

[11]He answered them, "He who made me well said to me, 'Take up your bed and walk.' "

[12]Then they asked him, "Who is the Man who said to you, 'Take up your bed and walk'?" [13]But the one who was healed did not know who it was, for Jesus had withdrawn, a multitude being in *that* place. [14]Afterward Jesus found him in the temple, and said to him, "See, you have been made well. Sin no more, lest a worse thing come upon you."

[15]The man departed and told the Jews that it was Jesus who had made him well.

Jesus Responds to His Critics

5:16–17
see pg. 346

5:17
see pg. 347

[16]For this reason the Jews persecuted Jesus, and sought to kill Him,[a] because He had done these things on the Sabbath. [17]But Jesus answered them, "My Father has been working until now, and I have been working."

5:2 [a]NU-Text reads *Bethzatha*.   5:4 [a]NU-Text omits *waiting for the moving of the water* at the end of verse 3, and all of verse 4.   5:16 [a]NU-Text omits *and sought to kill Him*.

• •

"You Can't Get Healed on the Sabbath!"

A CLOSER LOOK
5:8–18

Ever on the lookout for infractions of their traditions and especially eager to catch Jesus and His followers in sin, the Pharisees quibbled over a formerly lame man carrying his bed on the Sabbath (v. 10). Jesus' Sabbath-day miracles sparked no end of controversy with these legalists. But He refused to let their objections go unchallenged. See "Jesus Confronts the Legalists," Luke 6:1–11.

MYTH #3
10 MYTHS ABOUT CHRISTIANITY

(continued from previous page)

volve the local, temporary suspension of natural laws, will prove intolerable. But that is a nineteenth-century view of science. Few scientists of stature today support such a view.

Moreover, the so-called "laws of nature" are not prescriptive but *descriptive*. They do not determine what may happen; they describe what normally does happen. Therefore, science can legitimately say that miracles do not usually occur in nature. But it would be illegitimate to claim that miracles are impossible. Such a claim speaks outside the limits of science. If God has really come into this world in Christ, is it so surprising that He would perform miracles, as the Gospels report?

Science is not in conflict with Christianity. To be sure, some scientists are. But other scientists are passionately committed Christians, just like people in other walks of life. There are reasons why people choose for or against Christ, but those reasons are found elsewhere than in science. ◆

DOES GOD WORK ON SUNDAYS?

CONSIDER THIS 5:16–17 **Jesus offered an odd retort to His critics in the controversy over observance of the Sabbath (vv. 16–17). Genesis 2:2–3 said that God "rested" from His work on the seventh day of creation and "sanctified" it, or set it apart as something special. Later, the third of the Ten Commandments made the seventh day a holy day, a Sabbath or day of rest in Israel (Ex. 20:8–11). Many Christians continue this practice today (on Sundays).**

According to rabbinical legal tradition, the healed man was violating the Sabbath rest by carrying his bed (v. 10), as was Jesus by healing him on that day (v. 16). But Jesus said that even God "breaks" His own Sabbath by continuing to work (v. 17). Even though He has completed the Creation, He continues to maintain it and provide for His creatures—even on Sundays.

The point was that it's never the wrong day to do good.

18Therefore the Jews sought all the more to kill Him, because He not only broke the Sabbath, but also said that God was His Father, making Himself equal with God. 19Then Jesus answered and said to them, "Most assuredly, I say to you, the Son can do nothing of Himself, but what He sees the Father do; for whatever He does, the Son also does in like manner. 20For the Father loves the Son, and shows Him all things that He Himself does; and He will show Him greater works than these, that you may marvel. 21For as the Father raises the dead and gives life to *them,* even so the Son gives life to whom He will. 22For the Father judges no one, but has committed all judgment to the Son, 23that all should honor the Son just as they honor the Father. He who does not honor the Son does not honor the Father who sent Him.

24"Most assuredly, I say to you, he who hears My word and believes in Him who sent Me has everlasting life, and shall not come into judgment, but has passed from death into life. 25Most assuredly, I say to you, the hour is coming, and now is, when the dead will hear the voice of the Son of God; and those who hear will live. 26For as the Father has life in Himself, so He has granted the Son to have life in Himself, 27and has given Him authority to execute judgment also, because He is the Son of Man. 28Do not marvel at this; for the hour is coming in which all who are in the graves will hear His voice 29and come forth—those who have done good, to the resurrection of life, and those who have done evil, to the resurrection of condemnation. 30I can of Myself do nothing. As I hear, I judge; and My judgment is righteous, because I do not seek My own will but the will of the Father who sent Me.

31"If I bear witness of Myself, My witness is not true. 32There is another who bears witness of Me, and I know that the witness which He witnesses of Me is true. 33You have sent to John, and he has borne witness to the truth. 34Yet I do not receive testimony from man, but I say these things that you may be saved. 35He was the burning and shining lamp, and you were willing for a time to rejoice in his light. 36But I have a greater witness than John's; for the works which the Father has given Me to finish—the very works that I do—bear witness of Me, that the Father has sent Me. 37And the Father Himself, who sent Me, has testified of Me. You have neither heard His voice at any time, nor seen His form. 38But you do not have His word abiding in you, because whom He sent, Him you do not believe. 39You search the Scriptures, for in them you think you have eternal life; and these are they which testify of Me. 40But you are not willing to come to Me that you may have life.

(*Bible text continued on page 348*)

GOD—THE ORIGINAL WORKER

God is a worker! Perhaps you've never thought of Him that way. But that's how He first appears in Scripture. In the creation account (Gen. 1–2) He wears no end of occupational hats: strategic planner, designer, civil engineer, real estate developer, project manager, artist, and many more. Using these skills, He created something that was "very good" (1:31). How good? As good as God! No wonder the creation is said to "glorify," or praise God. His work is worth honoring, and it honors Him. (See Is. 43:7; 60:21.)

Furthermore, God continues to work (John 5:17), maintaining the creation and providing for His creatures. He also carries out the work of salvation. And He uses people to help Him accomplish these tasks. Think what that means:

(1) *Work itself is inherently good.* God didn't mind "getting His hands dirty," so to speak, in creating the universe. Genesis says He "worked" to bring it into existence (2:2). But that means work must be good in and of itself, since by definition, God can only do what is good. It also means work reflects the activity of God. The engineer who designs a bridge, the zoologist who studies animals, and the farmer who raises crops all carry out jobs that God did at the beginning of the world.

(2) *Your work is important; it matters.* The work that God gives you has dignity to it. In fact, God created you "in His image" (Gen. 1:26–27). Just as He works, so He has created you to work. Genesis even says that God has placed human beings in authority over the creation as His managers. As you use the abilities He's given you, you can be a partner, a coworker with Him to carry out His work.

For example, God can use: the nurse to meet the health needs of patients; the grocer to distribute food to customers; the researcher to provide accurate information; the lawyer to promote justice for clients; the career homemaker to nurture growing children. God values these kinds of jobs because they help to carry out His purposes in the world. These things matter to Him.

(3) *There's no such thing as "secular" or "sacred" work.* God certainly uses ministers and missionaries to meet spiritual and personal needs around the world. But they are not the only people doing "God's work." God is just as interested in the physical, emotional, intellectual, and other needs that people have. He also cares about the management of the earth itself. It takes all kinds of skills, and all kinds of people, to do what God wants done in the world.

(4) *You should do your work in a way that honors God.* Your work has dignity; you're created in God's image as a worker; you're a coworker with God; you have God-given abilities to carry out important tasks that He wants done. All of this says that what you do for work and how you do it should bring glory to God. He should be pleased with it—and with you as you do it. ◆

Our work isn't exactly the same as God's work, is it? See "Creation: 'Very Good,' But Not Sacred!" Heb. 11:3.

Doesn't Genesis say that God "rested" from His work? See "Does God Work on Sundays?" John 5:16–17.

Many people assume that work is a part of the curse. Is it? See Rom. 8:20–22.

[41]"I do not receive honor from men. [42]But I know you, that you do not have the love of God in you. [43]I have come in My Father's name, and you do not receive Me; if another comes in his own name, him you will receive. [44]How can you believe, who receive honor from one another, and do not seek the honor that *comes* from the only God? [45]Do not think that I shall accuse you to the Father; there is *one* who accuses you—Moses, in whom you trust. [46]For if you believed Moses, you would believe Me; for he wrote about Me. [47]But if you do not believe his writings, how will you believe My words?"

CHAPTER 6

Jesus Feeds 5,000

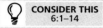 6:1–14   [1]After these things Jesus went over the Sea of Galilee, which is *the Sea* of Tiberias. [2]Then a great multitude followed Him, because they saw His signs which He performed on those who were diseased. [3]And Jesus went up on the mountain, and there He sat with His disciples.

[4]Now the Passover, a feast of the Jews, was near. [5]Then Jesus lifted up *His* eyes, and seeing a great multitude coming toward Him, He said to Philip, "Where shall we buy bread, that these may eat?" [6]But this He said to test him, for He Himself knew what He would do.

[7]Philip answered Him, "Two hundred denarii worth of bread is not sufficient for them, that every one of them may have a little."

[8]One of His disciples, Andrew, Simon Peter's brother, said to Him, [9]"There is a lad here who has five barley loaves and two small fish, but what are they among so many?"

[10]Then Jesus said, "Make the people sit down." Now there was much grass in the place. So the men sat down, in number about five thousand. [11]And Jesus took the loaves, and when He had given thanks He distributed *them* to the disciples, and the disciples[a] to those sitting down; and likewise of the fish, as much as they wanted. [12]So when they were filled, He said to His disciples, "Gather up the fragments that remain, so that nothing is lost." [13]Therefore they gathered *them* up, and filled twelve baskets with the fragments of the five barley loaves which were left over by those who had eaten. [14]Then those men, when they had seen the sign that Jesus did, said, "This is truly the Prophet who is to come into the world."

6:14–15

Jesus Walks on Water

6:15–21   [15]Therefore when Jesus perceived that they were about to come and take Him

6:11 [a]NU-Text omits *to the disciples, and the disciples.*

The Seven Signs of John's Gospel

FEEDING THE 5,000

💡 **CONSIDER THIS** 6:1–14   John writes that the crowd that followed Jesus did so in response to His miracles (v. 2), a link to the healing of the lame man in John 5:1–17. This leads to a fourth sign miracle, the feeding of the 5,000.

What Jesus did was remarkable in every way. Consider, for example, that even today very few facilities in the United States can accommodate 5,000 people for a sit-down meal. Yet Jesus miraculously provided for at least that many—with leftovers! John mentions that they filled twelve baskets—perhaps one for each disciple, or perhaps one for each of the twelve tribes of Israel. The overall result was faith: Jesus must be the Messiah, the crowd concluded (v. 14).

Yet doubt and rejection were soon to follow. Detractors pointed out that Jesus' lunch may have been impressive, but it was only one meal. By contrast, Moses had fed Israel in the wilderness for 40 years (vv. 30–31). Incredibly, they had missed the point of the sign: Jesus was not merely a deliveryman, He was the bread of life itself (vv. 32–58).

by force to make Him king, He departed again to the mountain by Himself alone.

¹⁶Now when evening came, His disciples went down to the sea, ¹⁷got into the boat, and went over the sea toward Capernaum. And it was already dark, and Jesus had not come to them. ¹⁸Then the sea arose because a great wind was blowing. ¹⁹So when they had rowed about three or four miles,ᵃ they saw Jesus walking on the sea and drawing near the boat; and they were afraid. ²⁰But He said to them, "It is I; do not be afraid." ²¹Then they willingly received Him into the boat, and immediately the boat was at the land where they were going.

"I Am the Bread of Life"

²²On the following day, when the people who were standing on the other side of the sea saw that there was no other boat there, except that one which His disciples had entered,ᵃ and that Jesus had not entered the boat with His disciples, but His disciples had gone away alone— ²³however, other boats came from Tiberias, near the place where they ate bread after the Lord had given thanks— ²⁴when the people therefore saw that Jesus was not there, nor His disciples, they also got into boats and came to Capernaum, seeking Jesus. ²⁵And when they found Him on the other side of the sea, they said to Him, "Rabbi, when did You come here?"

²⁶Jesus answered them and said, "Most assuredly, I say to you, you seek Me, not because you saw the signs, but because you ate of the loaves and were filled. ²⁷Do not labor for the food which perishes, but for the food which endures to everlasting life, which the Son of Man will give you, because God the Father has set His seal on Him."

²⁸Then they said to Him, "What shall we do, that we may work the works of God?"

²⁹Jesus answered and said to them, "This is the work of God, that you believe in Him whom He sent."

³⁰Therefore they said to Him, "What sign will You perform then, that we may see it and believe You? What work will You do? ³¹Our fathers ate the manna in the desert; as it is written, 'He gave them bread from heaven to eat.' "ᵃ

³²Then Jesus said to them, "Most assuredly, I say to you, Moses did not give you the bread from heaven, but My Father gives you the true bread from heaven. ³³For the bread of God is He who comes down from heaven and gives life to the world."

³⁴Then they said to Him, "Lord, give us this bread always."

6:19 ᵃLiterally *twenty-five or thirty stadia*   6:22 ᵃNU-Text omits *that* and *which His disciples had entered.*   6:31 ᵃExodus 16:4; Nehemiah 9:15; Psalm 78:24

PREVENTING KINGDOM CONFUSION

 CONSIDER THIS 6:14–15 **Throughout history people have longed for leaders to whom they can attach themselves. They often tie their own aspirations to the charisma and vision of a famous person, using that person to achieve their own ends, which are sometimes quite incompatible.**

Jesus knew the pattern well. He came to accomplish the work that His Father had given Him. But others quickly attached their own agendas and values to His plans (v. 15). Jesus resisted the mixed intentions of some of His followers and admirers because His kingdom differed fundamentally from their expectations.

What exactly was Jesus' concept of the kingdom, and what difference does it make for people today? See "The King Declares His Kingdom," Matt. 4:17.

The Seven Signs of John's Gospel

MIRACLES AT SEA

CONSIDER THIS 6:15–21 *The fifth sign miracle that John included in his Gospel was a private affair for the disciples alone (vv. 15–21). What happened on the troubled Sea of Galilee revealed Jesus as master of the elements. John makes no explanatory comment on this incident, but its impact on the disciples is evident in Peter's words: "We have come to believe and know that You are the Christ, the Son of the living God" (v. 69, emphasis added).*

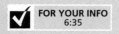 **6:35**

[35]And Jesus said to them, "I am the bread of life. He who comes to Me shall never hunger, and he who believes in Me shall never thirst. [36]But I said to you that you have seen Me and yet do not believe. [37]All that the Father gives Me will come to Me, and the one who comes to Me I will by no means cast out. [38]For I have come down from heaven, not to do My own will, but the will of Him who sent Me. [39]This is the will of the Father who sent Me, that of all He has given Me I should lose nothing, but should raise it up at the last day. [40]And this is the will of Him who sent Me, that everyone who sees the Son and believes in Him may have everlasting life; and I will raise him up at the last day."

Jesus' Listeners Are Confounded

[41]The Jews then complained about Him, because He said, "I am the bread which came down from heaven." [42]And they said, "Is not this Jesus, the son of Joseph, whose father and mother we know? How is it then that He says, 'I have come down from heaven'?"

[43]Jesus therefore answered and said to them, "Do not

FOR YOUR INFO
6:35

THE BREAD OF LIFE

When Jesus called Himself the "bread of life" (v. 35; also vv. 32–33, 41, 48), He was using as an image more than a staple of the diet, He was drawing on a rich symbol of Jewish life.

Bread played an important role in Israel's worship. During the celebration of Pentecost, two loaves of leavened bread were offered as sacrifices (Lev. 23:17). In the tabernacle, and later in the temple, the Levites placed twelve loaves of unleavened bread, or bread without yeast, before the Lord each week to symbolize God's presence with the twelve tribes (Ex. 25:30).

Throughout the Exodus, God miraculously sustained His people by sending manna from heaven each morning (Ex. 16). The bread-like manna was a "small round substance as fine as frost" (v. 14). It looked "like white coriander seed" and tasted like "wafers made with honey" (v. 31) or "pastry prepared with oil" (Num. 11:8).

It was this manna that Jesus was recalling when He called Himself "the true bread from heaven" (John 6:32), "the bread which came down from heaven" (6:41), and the "bread of life" (vv. 48–51, 58). Symbolically, Jesus is the heavenly manna, the spiritual or supernatural food given by the Father to those who ask, seek, and knock (v. 45; Matt. 7:7–8).

murmur among yourselves. ⁴⁴No one can come to Me unless the Father who sent Me draws him; and I will raise him up at the last day. ⁴⁵It is written in the prophets, 'And they shall all be taught by God.'ᵃ Therefore everyone who has heard and learnedᵇ from the Father comes to Me. ⁴⁶Not that anyone has seen the Father, except He who is from God; He has seen the Father. ⁴⁷Most assuredly, I say to you, he who believes in Meᵃ has everlasting life. ⁴⁸I am the bread of life. ⁴⁹Your fathers ate the manna in the wilderness, and are dead. ⁵⁰This is the bread which comes down from heaven, that one may eat of it and not die. ⁵¹I am the living bread which came down from heaven. If anyone eats of this bread, he will live forever; and the bread that I shall give is My flesh, which I shall give for the life of the world."

⁵²The Jews therefore quarreled among themselves, saying, "How can this Man give us *His* flesh to eat?"

⁵³Then Jesus said to them, "Most assuredly, I say to you, unless you eat the flesh of the Son of Man and drink His

6:45 ᵃIsaiah 54:13 ᵇM-Text reads *hears and has learned.* 6:47 ᵃNU-Text omits *in Me.*

◆ ◆ ◆ ◆ ◆ ◆ ◆ ◆ ◆ ◆ ◆ ◆ ◆ ◆ ◆ ◆ ◆ ◆ ◆

However, it's also interesting that Jesus' "bread of life discourse" (as John 6:26–58 is called) was given during Passover, also known as the Feast of Unleavened Bread (vv. 4, 22; see "Passover," Luke 22:7). Passover celebrated the deliverance of Israel from slavery in Egypt. On the night before leaving Egypt, the Israelites made unleavened bread, as they had no time to let their bread rise before taking flight (Ex. 12:8; 13:6–7).

In this context, Jesus had just fed at least 5,000 people (John 6:1–14), an event that led directly to the bread of life discourse (vv. 22–27). Clearly, He was indicating that He was God's provision for the people's deepest spiritual needs. Just as God had provided for His people as they came out of Egypt, so Jesus had provided physical food for the 5,000 and was ready to provide spiritual nourishment and life to all of them as well.

Tragically, the people balked at His teaching (vv. 30–31, 41–42, 52, 60). Their hearts were hardened in unbelief. Soon, many began to turn away (v. 66). But to those who believed, like Peter who declared, "You are the Christ, the Son of the Living God" (v. 69), Jesus gave abundant and eternal life. ◆

YOU ALONE CAN'T BRING THEM TO JESUS

CONSIDER THIS 6:44 **Do you stagger under a heavy load of expectation that you alone (or that you primarily) are responsible for bringing your friends and coworkers to faith? Do you feel guilty because you can't get them converted? If so, you may be surprised to discover that not even Jesus felt that kind of load for the lost!**

While explaining how people enter the kingdom, Jesus clearly declared that it is God the Father who draws them (v. 44). That means that people's response to the gospel does not depend primarily on you or on Jesus. Elsewhere, Jesus taught that:

- **"All that the Father gives Me will come to Me" (v. 37).**
- **"No one can come to Me unless it has been granted to him by My Father" (v. 65).**

Clearly, the responsibility for conversion ultimately belongs to the Father. Then is there anything we can do as Christ's followers to motivate others toward the Savior? Yes, we can give evidence of how God works in our lives as we grow. We can offer clear, truthful information about the gospel as we have opportunity. And we can invite and even urge others to believe.

But the ultimate responsibility for salvation is God's, not ours. So relax! Live the faith, talk about it, and offer it to others. But let the dynamic of conversion be from God alone.

Unfortunately, some believers run to the other extreme: they fold their hands and shut their mouths when it comes to evangelism. After all, it's up to God to bring people to faith. Is that what Jesus intended? See "Whose Job Is Evangelism?" John 16:8.

blood, you have no life in you. [54]Whoever eats My flesh and drinks My blood has eternal life, and I will raise him up at the last day. [55]For My flesh is food indeed,[a] and My blood is drink indeed. [56]He who eats My flesh and drinks My blood abides in Me, and I in him. [57]As the living Father sent Me, and I live because of the Father, so he who feeds on Me will live because of Me. [58]This is the bread which came down from heaven—not as your fathers ate the manna, and are dead. He who eats this bread will live forever."

[59]These things He said in the synagogue as He taught in Capernaum.

Many Followers Abandon Jesus

6:60–67 [60]Therefore many of His disciples, when they heard *this,* said, "This is a hard saying; who can understand it?"

[61]When Jesus knew in Himself that His disciples complained about this, He said to them, "Does this offend you? [62]*What* then if you should see the Son of Man ascend where He was before? [63]It is the Spirit who gives life; the flesh profits nothing. The words that I speak to you are spirit, and *they* are life. [64]But there are some of you who do not believe." For Jesus knew from the beginning who they were who did not believe, and who would betray Him. [65]And He said, "Therefore I have said to you that no one can come to Me unless it has been granted to him by My Father."

[66]From that *time* many of His disciples went back and walked with Him no more. [67]Then Jesus said to the twelve, "Do you also want to go away?"

Peter Declares that Jesus Is the Christ

[68]But Simon Peter answered Him, "Lord, to whom shall we go? You have the words of eternal life. [69]Also we have come to believe and know that You are the Christ, the Son of the living God."[a]

[70]Jesus answered them, "Did I not choose you, the twelve, and one of you is a devil?" [71]He spoke of Judas Iscariot, *the son* of Simon, for it was he who would betray Him, being one of the twelve.

6:55 [a]NU-Text reads *true food* and *true drink.*   6:69 [a]NU-Text reads *You are the Holy One of God.*

> "**H**E WHO FEEDS ON ME WILL LIVE BECAUSE OF ME."
> —John 6:57

The Desertion of the Disciples

A CLOSER LOOK 6:60–67 *Jesus attracted large crowds, and from them quite a number of disciples or "learners." However, when His teaching became costly and hard to accept (v. 60), many deserted Him—but not all. To find out more about these dedicated followers, see "The Twelve," Matt. 10:2, and "The Women Who Followed Jesus," Luke 8:1–3.*

CHAPTER 7

Jesus' Brothers Doubt Him

¹After these things Jesus walked in Galilee; for He did not want to walk in Judea, because the Jews*a* sought to kill Him. ²Now the Jews' Feast of Tabernacles was at hand. ³His brothers therefore said to Him, "Depart from here and go into Judea, that Your disciples also may see the works that You are doing. ⁴For no one does anything in secret while he himself seeks to be known openly. If You do these things, show Yourself to the world." ⁵For even His brothers did not believe in Him.

[🔍 7:2]

[💡 7:5]

⁶Then Jesus said to them, "My time has not yet come, but your time is always ready. ⁷The world cannot hate you, but it hates Me because I testify of it that its works are evil. ⁸You go up to this feast. I am not yet*a* going up to this feast, for My time has not yet fully come." ⁹When He had said these things to them, He remained in Galilee.

Jesus Attends the Feast of Tabernacles

¹⁰But when His brothers had gone up, then He also went up to the feast, not openly, but as it were in secret. ¹¹Then the Jews sought Him at the feast, and said, "Where is He?" ¹²And there was much complaining among the people concerning Him. Some said, "He is good"; others said, "No, on the contrary, He deceives the people." ¹³However, no one spoke openly of Him for fear of the Jews.

¹⁴Now about the middle of the feast Jesus went up into the temple and taught. ¹⁵And the Jews marveled, saying, "How does this Man know letters, having never studied?"

¹⁶Jesus*a* answered them and said, "My doctrine is not Mine, but His who sent Me. ¹⁷If anyone wills to do His will, he shall know concerning the doctrine, whether it is from God or *whether* I speak on My own *authority*. ¹⁸He who speaks from himself seeks his own glory; but He who seeks the glory of the One who sent Him is true, and no unrighteousness is in Him. ¹⁹Did not Moses give you the law, yet none of you keeps the law? Why do you seek to kill Me?"

7:1 *a*That is, the ruling authorities   7:8 *a*NU-Text omits *yet.*   7:16 *a*NU-Text and M-Text read *So Jesus.*

. . . .

The Feast of Tabernacles

[🔍 A CLOSER LOOK 7:2] The Feast of Tabernacles (v. 2) was one of three great feast days in the life of the Hebrews. It offered Jesus an ideal moment of opportunity in which to declare Himself publicly. See "Jewish Feasts," Luke 2:42, and "'We Interrupt This Program . . . ,'" John 7:37.

DOES ANYONE BELIEVE YOU?

[💡 CONSIDER THIS 7:5] If you ever feel discouraged because family, friends, or coworkers refuse to accept the gospel, you may take some comfort from the fact that even Jesus' own brothers did not believe that He was the Christ (v. 5). Even though they had seen His miracles and listened to His teaching, they still balked at the idea of placing faith in Jesus as the Son of God.

This is important to notice, because it shows that the person who hears the gospel bears responsibility for responding in faith, while the person who shares the gospel bears responsibility for communicating with faithfulness. If we as believers ever start holding ourselves responsible for whether unbelievers accept or reject the message of Christ, we are headed for trouble!

That's not to suggest that we can be careless in our witness or ignore our credibility. Notice that Jesus' brothers rejected Him *in spite of* His works and words. Is that true of us? Or do people dismiss our faith because our lives show little evidence that what we say we believe is true or that it makes any difference to us?

Eventually, at least some of Jesus' brothers did believe in Him. James, probably the oldest, became a leader in the church (Acts 15:13–21) and wrote the New Testament letter that bears his name. Likewise, the author of Jude may have been the half-brother of Jesus. Ultimately, both urged Christians to practice and defend their *faith* (James 2:2–26; Jude 3).

Maybe you have decided that since it's up to God to bring people to faith, you can relax and keep quiet about the gospel. Is that a realistic attitude? See "Whose Job Is Evangelism?" John 16:8.

²⁰The people answered and said, "You have a demon. Who is seeking to kill You?"

²¹Jesus answered and said to them, 7:21–24 "I did one work, and you all marvel. ²²Moses therefore gave you circumcision (not that it is from Moses, but from the fathers), and you circumcise a man on the Sabbath. ²³If a man receives circumcision on the Sabbath, so that the law of Moses should not be broken, are you angry with Me because I made a man completely well on the Sabbath? ²⁴Do not judge according to appearance, but judge with righteous judgment."

²⁵Now some of them from Jerusalem said, "Is this not He whom they seek to kill? ²⁶But look! He speaks boldly, and they say nothing to Him. Do the rulers know indeed that this is truly*ᵃ* the Christ? ²⁷However, we know where this Man is from; but when the Christ comes, no one knows where He is from."

²⁸Then Jesus cried out, as He taught in the temple, saying, "You both know Me, and you know where I am from; and I have not come of Myself, but He who sent Me is true, whom you do not know. ²⁹But*ᵃ* I know Him, for I am from Him, and He sent Me."

³⁰Therefore they sought to take Him; but no one laid a hand on Him, because His hour had not yet come. ³¹And many of the people believed in Him, and said, "When the Christ comes, will He do more signs than these which this *Man* has done?"

³²The Pharisees heard the crowd murmuring these things concerning Him, and the Pharisees and the chief priests sent officers to take Him. ³³Then Jesus said to them,*ᵃ* "I shall be with you a little while longer, and *then* I go to Him who sent Me. ³⁴You will seek Me and not find *Me,* and where I am you cannot come."

³⁵Then the Jews said among themselves, "Where does He intend to go that we shall not find Him? Does He intend to go to the Dispersion among the Greeks and teach the Greeks? ³⁶What is this thing that He said, 'You will seek Me and not find Me, and where I am you cannot come'?"

7:26 ªNU-Text omits *truly.*   7:29 ªNU-Text and M-Text omit *But.*   7:33 ªNU-Text and M-Text omit *to them.*

> ## "DO NOT JUDGE ACCORDING TO APPEARANCE BUT JUDGE WITH RIGHTEOUS JUDGMENT."
> —John 7:24

Blind Guides

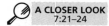 A CLOSER LOOK 7:21–24 *The Pharisees had grown so out of touch with the intent of the Law that they could no longer distinguish between appearance and reality. Jesus challenged them by appealing to the very Scriptures they held so dear (vv. 22–23). Here as elsewhere, He refused to let them abuse Him or others with their hypocrisy. See "Jesus Confronts the Legalists," Luke. 6:1–11.*

Jesus Provides Living Water

7:37
see pg. 356

³⁷On the last day, that great *day* of the feast, Jesus stood and cried out, saying, "If anyone thirsts, let him come to Me and drink. ³⁸He who believes in Me, as the Scripture has said, out of his heart will flow rivers of living water." ³⁹But this He spoke concerning the Spirit, whom those believing[a] in Him would receive; for the Holy[b] Spirit was not yet *given,* because Jesus was not yet glorified.

⁴⁰Therefore many[a] from the crowd, when they heard this saying, said, "Truly this is the Prophet." ⁴¹Others said, "This is the Christ."

But some said, "Will the Christ come out of Galilee? ⁴²Has not the Scripture said that the Christ comes from the seed of David and from the town of Bethlehem, where David was?" ⁴³So there was a division among the people because of Him. ⁴⁴Now some of them wanted to take Him, but no one laid hands on Him.

⁴⁵Then the officers came to the chief priests and Pharisees, who said to them, "Why have you not brought Him?"

⁴⁶The officers answered, "No man ever spoke like this Man!"

⁴⁷Then the Pharisees answered them, "Are you also deceived? ⁴⁸Have any of the rulers or the Pharisees believed in Him? ⁴⁹But this crowd that does not know the law is accursed."

⁵⁰Nicodemus (he who came to Jesus by night,[a] being one of them) said to them, ⁵¹"Does our law judge a man before it hears him and knows what he is doing?"

7:52

⁵²They answered and said to him, "Are you also from Galilee? Search and look, for no prophet has arisen[a] out of Galilee."

⁵³And everyone went to his *own* house.[a]

CHAPTER 8

¹But Jesus went to the Mount of Olives.

A Woman Caught in Adultery

8:2–3

²Now early[a] in the morning He came again into the temple, and all the people

7:39 [a]NU-Text reads *who believed.* [b]NU-Text omits *Holy.* 7:40 [a]NU-Text reads *some.* 7:50 [a]NU-Text reads *before.* 7:52 [a]NU-Text reads *is to rise.* 7:53 [a]The words *And everyone* through *sin no more* (8:11) are bracketed by NU-Text as not original. They are present in over 900 manuscripts. 8:2 [a]M-Text reads *very early.*

• •

No Prophet from Galilee

A CLOSER LOOK
7:52

Pharisees and other citizens of Judea looked upon their brothers from Galilee with scorn. To them, a "Galilean" was a fool, heathen, sinner, or worse. See "Jesus the Galilean," Mark 1:14.

A DOUBLE STANDARD?

CONSIDER THIS
8:2–3

The woman presented to Jesus (v. 3) must have been utterly humiliated at being dragged into the temple by self-righteous men who were only using her to try to trick the Teacher they hated. According to the Law, adultery required capital punishment of *both* parties (Lev. 20:10). Did the accusers forget to bring the man? Or had they allowed a double standard to creep in?

If so, Jesus refrained from challenging their hypocrisy, but He did set a new standard for judgment: Let someone perfect decide the case (v. 7; compare Matt. 5:48). Ironically, He was the only one who fit that qualification, and He did decide the case—declining to condemn the woman, but admonishing her to "go and sin no more."

Are there double standards in your moral judgments? Are you eager to point out the speck in someone else's eye, while ignoring the plank in your own (Matt. 7:4–5)? Or, perhaps, like the woman, you've experienced the forgiveness of God for grave offenses against His holiness. If so, live in His grace—and sin no more.

came to Him; and He sat down and taught them. ³Then the scribes and Pharisees brought to Him a woman caught in adultery. And when they had set her in the midst, ⁴they said to Him, "Teacher, this woman was caught*ᵃ* in adultery, in the very act. ⁵Now Moses, in the law, commanded*ᵃ* us that such should be stoned.*ᵇ* But what do You say?"*ᶜ* ⁶This they said, testing Him, that they might have *something* of which to accuse Him. But Jesus stooped down and wrote on the ground with *His* finger, as though He did not hear.*ᵃ*

⁷So when they continued asking Him, He raised Himself up*ᵃ* and said to them, "He who is without sin among you, let him throw a stone at her first." ⁸And again He stooped down and wrote on the ground. ⁹Then those who heard *it,* being convicted by *their* conscience,*ᵃ* went out one by one,

8:4 ᵃM-Text reads *we found this woman.*   8:5 ᵃM-Text reads *in our law Moses commanded.*   ᵇNU-Text and M-Text read *to stone such.*   ᶜM-Text adds *about her.*
8:6 ᵃNU-Text and M-Text omit *as though He did not hear.*   8:7 ᵃM-Text reads *He looked up.*   8:9 ᵃNU-Text and M-Text omit *being convicted by their conscience.*

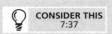

CONSIDER THIS
7:37

"WE INTERRUPT THIS PROGRAM . . ."

Jesus' cry in v. 37 was far more dramatic than most modern readers realize. He chose a time when Jerusalem was packed with holiday visitors and a crucial moment in the festivities when He could attract the most attention. It would be as if someone broke into the broadcast of a presidential state-of-the-union address or the kickoff of a Super Bowl to announce, "We interrupt this program to bring you a special report."

The annual Feast of Tabernacles (or Booths, or Tents, 7:2) swelled Jerusalem with an overflow of festive crowds. Every Jewish family within 20 miles of the city was required to move out of its home and live in a booth or tent in remembrance of Israel's wanderings in the wilderness. Many chose to move into the city for the week. Reunions and parties alternated with solemn processions from the temple down to the Pool of Siloam, a reservoir (9:7). Pushing its way through the crowded streets, the throng sang Psalms 113 to 118 in anticipation of God's righteous reign over Jerusalem.

Jesus chose to keep a low profile at this year's festival (7:2–10). He taught in the temple (v. 14), but waited for the right moment to declare Himself publicly. It came on the last day of the feast (v. 37), probably at the climax of the daily processional.

As on the previous six days, the high priest filled a goblet of water from Siloam and carried it back to the beginning with the oldest *even* to the last. And Jesus was left alone, and the woman standing in the midst. [10]When Jesus had raised Himself up and saw no one but the woman, He said to her,[a] "Woman, where are those accusers of yours?[b] Has no one condemned you?"

[11]She said, "No one, Lord."

And Jesus said to her, "Neither do I condemn you; go and[a] sin no more."

"I Am the Light of the World"

[12]Then Jesus spoke to them again, saying, "I am the light of the world. He who follows Me shall not walk in darkness, but have the light of life."

[13]The Pharisees therefore said to Him, "You bear witness of Yourself; Your witness is not true."

8:10 [a]NU-Text omits *and saw no one but the woman;* M-Text reads *He saw her and said.* [b]NU-Text and M-Text omit *of yours.* 8:11 [a]NU-Text and M-Text add *from now on.*

temple, where he poured it out for all the people to see. Each day at that point the crowds chanted, "Oh, give thanks to the LORD" (Ps. 118:1), and "Save now, I pray, O LORD; O LORD, I pray, send now prosperity" (118:25), and again, "Oh, give thanks to the LORD." Then they shook myrtle, willow, and palm branches toward the altar, as if to remind God of His promises. Then, after a pause, sacrifices were offered.

On the last day, however, just after the crowds had not only waved their branches but, as was the custom, literally shook them to pieces in a frenzy of enthusiasm, a voice suddenly cried out: "If anyone thirsts, let him come to Me and drink" (John 7:37, emphasis added). Jesus' timing couldn't have been more perfect or His claim more explicit: He was declaring Himself to be none other than the long-awaited Christ who would pour out the Holy Spirit, as many in the crowd immediately recognized (vv. 39–43).

In many ways v. 37 acts as the pivot for John's account. From that point on, the hostility of Jesus' enemies mounted until they finally arrested Him (18:12) in vain hopes of shutting off the "living water." ◆

The Feast of Tabernacles was one of three major festivals for the Hebrews of Jesus' day. See "Jewish Feasts," Luke 2:42.

> **"HE WHO FOLLOWS ME SHALL NOT WALK IN DARKNESS, BUT HAVE THE LIGHT OF LIFE."**
> **—John 8:12**

¹⁴Jesus answered and said to them, "Even if I bear witness of Myself, My witness is true, for I know where I came from and where I am going; but you do not know where I come from and where I am going. ¹⁵You judge according to the flesh; I judge no one. ¹⁶And yet if I do judge, My judgment is true; for I am not alone, but I *am* with the Father who sent Me. ¹⁷It is also written in your law that the testimony of two men is true. ¹⁸I am One who bears witness of Myself, and the Father who sent Me bears witness of Me."

¹⁹Then they said to Him, "Where is Your Father?"

Jesus answered, "You know neither Me nor My Father. If you had known Me, you would have known My Father also."

²⁰These words Jesus spoke in the treasury, as He taught in the temple; and no one laid hands on Him, for His hour had not yet come.

²¹Then Jesus said to them again, "I am going away, and

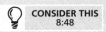

CONSIDER THIS
8:48

Jesus Is Called a Samaritan Demoniac

John 8 records a heated, even bitter, confrontation between Jesus and the Jews, led by the Pharisees. The Lord became particularly blunt with the religious leaders because they refused to accept His claims, imperiling not only their own spiritual standing but that of Israel.

EXCHANGE BETWEEN JESUS AND THE PHARISEES	
Jesus told the Pharisees...	**The Pharisees responded...**
I know where I came from and where I'm going (8:14–18).	You were born illegitimately (8:19).
You do not know God (8:19).	No response.
You will die in your sin (8:21, 24).	Who are You? (8:25).
[My] truth will make you free (8:31–32).	We've never needed freedom (8:33).
You are the slaves of sin (8:34–38).	We are children of Abraham (8:39).
You are murderers and liars, doing the deeds of your father (8:39–41).	We are not illegitimate [like You]; besides, God is our Father (8:41).
Your father is the devil, a murderer and liar (8:42–47).	You're nothing but a Samaritan and have a demon! (8:48).
I have power even over death (8:49–51).	Who do You think You are? (8:52–54).
My Father honors Me [as His Son]; but you are liars (8:54–56).	You're just a young upstart, yet You claim to have seen Abraham! (8:57).
I AM (8:58; compare Gen. 17:1; Ex. 3:14).	They picked up stones to throw at Him (8:59).

you will seek Me, and will die in your sin. Where I go you cannot come."

²²So the Jews said, "Will He kill Himself, because He says, 'Where I go you cannot come'?"

²³And He said to them, "You are from beneath; I am from above. You are of this world; I am not of this world. ²⁴Therefore I said to you that you will die in your sins; for if you do not believe that I am *He,* you will die in your sins."

²⁵Then they said to Him, "Who are You?"

And Jesus said to them, "Just what I have been saying to you from the beginning. ²⁶I have many things to say and to judge concerning you, but He who sent Me is true; and I speak to the world those things which I heard from Him."

²⁷They did not understand that He spoke to them of the Father.

²⁸Then Jesus said to them, "When you lift up the Son of

(Bible text continued on page 361)

Calling Jesus a demon-crazed Samaritan was about the most insulting thing His opponents could think to say. "Samaritan" and "demoniac" were virtual synonyms in their minds. The names expressed all of the bitterness, rage, and contempt they felt toward Jesus.

By the way, what names would people call you as you stand for God's truth at your job or in your community? What hate words would you cringe to hear? ◆

"**I**F YOU DO NOT BELIEVE THAT **I** AM **H**E, YOU WILL DIE IN YOUR SINS."
—**John 8:24**

Jews and Samaritans were deeply divided by ethnic barriers. In fact, they had almost no dealings with each other—not unlike many societies today. See John 4:4.

MANY MEN WOULD BE GODS, BUT ONLY ONE GOD WOULD BE MAN

History is crowded with men who claimed to be gods. Christianity is unique in that it reveals that the one God became man, in the person of Jesus Christ. That is the dramatic import of Jesus' words, "Before Abraham was, I AM" (v. 58). I AM was an expression by which God was known to the Hebrews (Ex. 3:14). In using such words, Jesus was declaring that God Himself was standing before the crowd.

By contrast, consider others in history who wanted their followers to regard them as gods, or who were given such adulation after they died:

King Tutankhamen

The boy king of Egypt, who reigned during the fourteenth century B.C., was regarded as a god. We know a lot about him since the discovery in 1922 of his tomb of gold. He died at 18.

Siddhartha Gautama

The first "Enlightened One," or *Buddha,* was born into royalty (c. 563–483 B.C.). However, he renounced all luxury and became a wandering ascetic searching for and later teaching a "middle way" to transcend the human condition. After his death, the Buddha was deified by his followers, who spread his teachings from India to southern and eastern Asia.

Alexander the Great

When the great military general of Macedonia overthrew the Persian Empire (c. 334–323 B.C.), he became a legend bigger than life. He attempted to fuse the Macedonians and the Persians into one master race of which he would be the supreme being. He demanded the same divine recognition from his subject people that they gave to the Greek gods, Heracles and Dionysus. Nevertheless, an illness claimed his life at age 33.

Julius Caesar

A Roman general and statesman, Caesar changed the course of the Graeco-Roman world by conquering Gaul (58–50 B.C.) and winning the Roman Civil War (49–45 B.C.). Crowned emperor, he had military and literary genius that was matched only by his carnal appetite. After his murder in 44 B.C. he was granted status as a god.

King Herod Agrippa I

The grandson of Herod the Great (see "The Herods," Acts 12:1–2) executed James the apostle and tried to do the same with Peter. Later, Agrippa's subjects in Tyre and Sidon, weary of his anger, attempted to make peace with him. Listening to one of his orations, they humored him by shouting, "The voice of a god and not of a man!" Apparently pleased with this sudden elevation in his status, he failed to correct their theology. God struck him for his arrogance so that he was eaten by worms and died (12:20–23).

Napoleon Bonaparte

The renowned French general and emperor made numerous reforms in government, education, and the military. The Napoleonic Code became a basis for civil law throughout the West. A military genius, he waged war and consolidated power throughout Europe (1800–1810). But he died in exile at age 51.

Vladimir Lenin

A militant Marxist, Lenin led the Bolshevik Revolution (1917)

(continued on next page)

Man, then you will know that I am *He*, and *that* I do nothing of Myself; but as My Father taught Me, I speak these things. ²⁹And He who sent Me is with Me. The Father has not left Me alone, for I always do those things that please Him." ³⁰As He spoke these words, many believed in Him.

³¹Then Jesus said to those Jews who believed Him, "If you abide in My word, you are My disciples indeed. ³²And you shall know the truth, and the truth shall make you free."

³³They answered Him, "We are Abraham's descendants, and have never been in bondage to anyone. How *can* You say, 'You will be made free'?"

³⁴Jesus answered them, "Most assuredly, I say to you, whoever commits sin is a slave of sin. ³⁵And a slave does not abide in the house forever, *but* a son abides forever. ³⁶Therefore if the Son makes you free, you shall be free indeed.

³⁷"I know that you are Abraham's descendants, but you seek to kill Me, because My word has no place in you. ³⁸I speak what I have seen with My Father, and you do what you have seen with^a your father."

³⁹They answered and said to Him, "Abraham is our father."

Jesus said to them, "If you were Abraham's children, you would do the works of Abraham. ⁴⁰But now you seek to kill Me, a Man who has told you the truth which I heard from God. Abraham did not do this. ⁴¹You do the deeds of your father."

Then they said to Him, "We were not born of fornication; we have one Father—God."

⁴²Jesus said to them, "If God were your Father, you would love Me, for I proceeded forth and came from God; nor have I come of Myself, but He sent Me. ⁴³Why do you not understand My speech? Because you are not able to listen to My word. ⁴⁴You are of *your* father the devil, and the desires of your father you want to do. He was a murderer from the beginning, and does not stand in the truth, because there is no truth in him. When he speaks a lie, he speaks from his own *resources,* for he is a liar and the father of it. ⁴⁵But because I tell the truth, you do not believe Me. ⁴⁶Which of you convicts Me of sin? And if I tell the truth, why do you not believe Me? ⁴⁷He who is of God hears God's words; therefore you do not hear, because you are not of God."

8:48
see pg. 358
⁴⁸Then the Jews answered and said to Him, "Do we not say rightly that You are a Samaritan and have a demon?"

⁴⁹Jesus answered, "I do not have a demon; but I honor My Father, and you dishonor Me. ⁵⁰And I do not seek My *own* glory; there is One who seeks and judges. ⁵¹Most as-

8:38 ^aNU-Text reads *heard from.*

(continued from previous page)

and became the first head of the former Soviet Union. His writings vastly expanded and promoted the Communist worldview, and he hoped they would stimulate other proletarian revolutions. He died at the age of 54 after a long, paralyzing illness. He was the closest thing to a "god" that the Soviets would allow. His body was put on view in Moscow.

Adolf Hitler

The mad dictator of Nazi Germany (1932–45) was unequaled in his ability to wield hypnotic power over masses of people. He knew how to manipulate events and people to his own ends, but his attempts to build a master race resulted only in a holocaust of evil. He died by his own hand in 1945.

Only Jesus Backed Up His Claim

Many more pretenders could be listed. But only Jesus demonstrated that He was God by His words and actions. He healed the sick, raised the dead, forgave sins, and lived by the moral precepts that He taught. In fact, He fulfilled every code of righteousness without ever sinning. Most importantly, He backed up His claim of being God by conquering death. No one else in history has ever done that. Others have been regarded as divine, but all have fallen short of God's glory—except Jesus. ◆

suredly, I say to you, if anyone keeps My word he shall never see death.”

 8:52–59
see pg. 360
⁵²Then the Jews said to Him, “Now we know that You have a demon! Abraham is dead, and the prophets; and You say, ‘If anyone keeps My word he shall never taste death.’ ⁵³Are You greater than our father Abraham, who is dead? And the prophets are dead. Who do You make Yourself out to be?”

⁵⁴Jesus answered, “If I honor Myself, My honor is nothing. It is My Father who honors Me, of whom you say that He is your*a* God. ⁵⁵Yet you have not known Him, but I know Him. And if I say, ‘I do not know Him,’ I shall be a liar like you; but I do know Him and keep His word. ⁵⁶Your father Abraham rejoiced to see My day, and he saw *it* and was glad.”

⁵⁷Then the Jews said to Him, “You are not yet fifty years old, and have You seen Abraham?”

⁵⁸Jesus said to them, “Most assuredly, I say to you, before Abraham was, I AM.”

⁵⁹Then they took up stones to throw at Him; but Jesus hid Himself and went out of the temple,*a* going through the midst of them, and so passed by.

CHAPTER 9

Jesus Heals a Man Born Blind

 9:1–41

 9:2–3

¹Now as *Jesus* passed by, He saw a man who was blind from birth. ²And His disciples asked Him, saying, “Rabbi, who sinned, this man or his parents, that he was born blind?”

³Jesus answered, “Neither this man nor his parents sinned, but that the works of God should be revealed in him. ⁴I*a* must work the works of Him who sent Me while it is day; *the* night is coming when no one can work. ⁵As long as I am in the world, I am the light of the world.”

⁶When He had said these things, He spat on the ground and made clay with the saliva; and He anointed the eyes of the blind man with the clay. ⁷And He said to him, “Go, wash in the pool of Siloam” (which is translated, Sent). So he went and washed, and came back seeing.

⁸Therefore the neighbors and those who previously had seen that he was blind*a* said, “Is not this he who sat and begged?”

⁹Some said, “This is he.” Others *said,* “He is like him.”*a*

(Bible text continued on page 364)

---

*8:54 *aNU-Text and M-Text read *our.*   *8:59 *aNU-Text omits the rest of this verse.
*9:4 *aNU-Text reads *We.*   *9:8 *aNU-Text reads *a beggar.*   *9:9 *aNU-Text reads *“No, but he is like him.”*

The Seven Signs of John's Gospel

JESUS HEALS THE BLIND MAN

 CONSIDER THIS
9:1–41
The sixth sign miracle featured in John's Gospel reveals Jesus as the light of the world (v. 5). He was also unique among the prophets in that none of them had cured blindness (vv. 30–33).

The healing of the blind man speaks to the problem of human suffering. Then as now, sickness was often assumed to be divine punishment for someone's sin. Like Job's counselors (Job 4:7–9; 8:2–8; 11:4–20), Jesus' disciples asked, “Whose sin caused this man's blindness?” (v. 2). But Jesus replied with a radically new truth: God can use human suffering to reveal His glory (v. 3). Jesus immediately showed what He was talking about by healing the man's blindness, thereby revealing Himself to be the Son of God.

"WHO SINNED?" HEALTH AND DISEASE IN THE BIBLE

When Jesus' disciples asked Him whose sin had caused a man's blindness (v. 2), they were reflecting a common perception about health and disease in the ancient world. In their minds, physical maladies and suffering were the result of sin and/or God's judgment.

Viewed from our perspective 2,000 years later, their question seems quaint and simplistic. Yet was it really? Even with all of our culture's medical technology, we still wrestle the same issue: what is the ultimate cause of sickness and death? We may understand the scientific explanations and even know how to prevent or cure countless ills. But we still look for a larger meaning behind physical health and disease.

The Bible mentions more than 40 specific diseases or disabilities and alludes frequently to sickness and health issues generally. It seems to accept that concerns about physical health are universal, inescapable, and problematic.

The Great Physician

Jesus devoted considerable time and teaching to health issues, provoking many questions in the process. The most challenging aspect of His work was the miracles of physical healing

that He performed. They confounded those who saw them first-hand no less than they trouble us today.

The Gospel writers make it clear that Jesus' first-century witnesses had no problem believing that He actually healed the sick and even raised the dead. They never accused Him of charlatanism. Apparently they accepted the miracles as miracles. But what they struggled with profoundly was the source of His power to perform them and the resulting implications. The curious wondered whether He might not be the Messiah (John 7:31); His enemies accused Him of being in league with the devil (8:48; 10:19–21; Matt. 9:34).

What most troubled people was that the miracles signaled the arrival of the kingdom of God. It was not the healings themselves that they anguished over, but what they were going to do with the One who claimed to be the Christ on the basis of

those healings. Was He or wasn't He? And were they ready to receive Him or not?

Modern Skepticism

Today our culture challenges the credibility of the miraculous itself. Capable of accomplishing many physical feats once thought to be "impossible" (flying, curing leprosy, seeing inside the body noninvasively), and lacking many (some would say any) current examples of miracles, skeptics look for some "rational" explanation. "Perhaps Jesus knew more about the body than the average first-century Jew and cleverly manipulated physical forces in a way that people assumed the miraculous," some say. "Perhaps He only appeared to heal, duping the simple like so many modern-day pretenders. Perhaps the miracles never really occurred; they were simply imagined by later believers eager to embellish the myth of a God-man."

Other explanations have been put forth in the last two centuries. They all reflect the skepticism of our age. Yet in the end, one comes out at the same place as those who originally challenged the authority of the miracles: "If I cast out demons by the

(continued on next page)

(continued from previous page)

Spirit of God, surely the kingdom of God has come upon you" (Matt. 12:28). In other words, is it really the possibility of miracles that troubles moderns? Or is it the staggering probability that the One who performed them is in fact God Himself? ◆

JESUS AND THE PHYSICAL

- Most of the healings that Jesus performed were intended to reveal His divine power and authority (John 9:2–3).
- He healed people from all walks of life, both the untouchables and the well-off and well-connected.
- He did not heal everyone (Matt. 13:58).
- He recognized and dealt with the emotional side of illness—feelings of sadness, anger, disorientation, anxiety, conflict, fear, and aggression.
- He exhibited patience, compassion, and courage when confronting the sick.
- He never used spells, charms, incantations, drugs, incense, or herbs to ward off evil spirits or to heal people of their diseases. His power came directly from His person.
- He drew a parallel between physical sickness and spiritual need (Mark 2:15–17).
- He often linked the healing of disease with faith and the forgiveness of sins.
- He refused to see all sickness as a sign of God's judgment.
- He refused to allow religious traditions and taboos to prevent Him from relieving pain and suffering.

(continued on next page)

He said, "I am *he*."

¹⁰Therefore they said to him, "How were your eyes opened?"

¹¹He answered and said, "A Man called Jesus made clay and anointed my eyes and said to me, 'Go to the pool of ͣ Siloam and wash.' So I went and washed, and I received sight."

¹²Then they said to him, "Where is He?"

He said, "I do not know."

¹³They brought him who formerly was blind to the Pharisees. ¹⁴Now it was a Sabbath when Jesus made the clay and opened his eyes. ¹⁵Then the Pharisees also asked him again how he had received his sight. He said to them, "He put clay on my eyes, and I washed, and I see."

¹⁶Therefore some of the Pharisees said, "This Man is not from God, because He does not keep the Sabbath."

Others said, "How can a man who is a sinner do such signs?" And there was a division among them.

¹⁷They said to the blind man again, "What do you say about Him because He opened your eyes?"

He said, "He is a prophet."

¹⁸But the Jews did not believe concerning him, that he had been blind and received his sight, until they called the parents of him who had received his sight. ¹⁹And they asked them, saying, "Is this your son, who you say was born blind? How then does he now see?"

²⁰His parents answered them and said, "We know that this is our son, and that he was born blind; ²¹but by what means he now sees we do not know, or who opened his eyes we do not know. He is of age; ask him. He will speak for himself." ²²His parents said these *things* because they feared the Jews, for the Jews had agreed already that if anyone confessed *that* He *was* Christ, he would be put out of the synagogue. ²³Therefore his parents said, "He is of age; ask him."

²⁴So they again called the man who was blind, and said to him, "Give God the glory! We know that this Man is a sinner."

²⁵He answered and said, "Whether He is a sinner *or not* I do not know. One thing I know: that though I was blind, now I see."

²⁶Then they said to him again, "What did He do to you? How did He open your eyes?"

²⁷He answered them, "I told you already, and you did not listen. Why do you want to hear *it* again? Do you also want to become His disciples?"

²⁸Then they reviled him and said, "You are His disciple, but we are Moses' disciples. ²⁹We know that God spoke to

9:11 ͣNU-Text omits *the pool of.*

Moses; *as for* this *fellow,* we do not know where He is from."

³⁰The man answered and said to them, "Why, this is a marvelous thing, that you do not know where He is from; yet He has opened my eyes! ³¹Now we know that God does not hear sinners; but if anyone is a worshiper of God and does His will, He hears him. ³²Since the world began it has been unheard of that anyone opened the eyes of one who was born blind. ³³If this Man were not from God, He could do nothing."

³⁴They answered and said to him, "You were completely born in sins, and are you teaching us?" And they cast him out.

³⁵Jesus heard that they had cast him out; and when He had found him, He said to him, "Do you believe in the Son of God?"ᵃ

³⁶He answered and said, "Who is He, Lord, that I may believe in Him?"

³⁷And Jesus said to him, "You have both seen Him and it is He who is talking with you."

³⁸Then he said, "Lord, I believe!" And he worshiped Him.

³⁹And Jesus said, "For judgment I have come into this world, that those who do not see may see, and that those who see may be made blind."

⁴⁰Then *some* of the Pharisees who were with Him heard these words, and said to Him, "Are we blind also?"

⁴¹Jesus said to them, "If you were blind, you would have no sin; but now you say, 'We see.' Therefore your sin remains."

CHAPTER 10

"I Am the Good Shepherd"

¹"Most assuredly, I say to you, he who does not enter the sheepfold by the door, but climbs up some other way, the same is a thief and a robber. ²But he who enters by the door is the shepherd of the sheep. ³To him the doorkeeper opens, and the sheep hear his voice; and he calls his own sheep by name and leads them out. ⁴And when he brings out his own sheep, he goes before them; and the sheep follow him, for they know his voice. ⁵Yet they will by no means follow a stranger, but will flee from him, for they do not know the voice of strangers." ⁶Jesus used this illustration, but they did not understand the things which He spoke to them.

⁷Then Jesus said to them again, "Most assuredly, I say to you, I am the door of the sheep. ⁸All who *ever* came before Meᵃ are thieves and robbers, but the sheep did not hear

9:35 ᵃNU-Text reads *Son of Man.* 10:8 ᵃM-Text omits *before Me.*

(continued from previous page)

- **His power to heal threatened the established authorities.**
- **His immediate followers experienced the same power over physical maladies, a sign that their message was from God.**
- **Sometimes illness and death showed God's judgment (Acts 5:1–11; 12:19–23).**
- **His followers were not spared from physical afflictions. God used their sufferings to form character.**
- **We can look forward to a time when suffering, sorrow, pain, and disease will come to an end (Rom. 8:18; Rev. 21:4).**

* * * * * * * * * * * * * * * *

Not only did healing demonstrate Christ's divine power over disease and infirmity, it revealed God's heart of compassion. "He Healed Them All" (Luke 4:40) lists some of the diseases and disabilities that Jesus and His followers treated.

THE POWER OF SELF-SACRIFICE

CONSIDER THIS 10:17–18 **What does power look like in the lives of people you know? Does it mean aggressively making things happen? Does it mean political or financial muscle? Jesus described His power as the right and ability to lay down His life for others (vv. 17–18).**

For whom or what would you lay down your life? Is there a cause so noble or people so dear that you would willingly let go of life itself? The world may not view that kind of self-sacrifice as power. But we who follow Christ can know the profound power of love—looking out not only for our own interests, but also for the interests of others (Phil. 2:4).

Jesus' first followers experienced a dynamic power that changed the world. See "Power," Acts 1:8.

THE FEAST OF DEDICATION

FOR YOUR INFO
10:22

The Feast of Dedication (v. 22) was a minor feast held in the Jewish month of Chislev (November-December). We know it today as Hanukkah, or the Feast of Lights. It was not a feast prescribed by Old Testament Law. Rather it originated as a celebration of the cleansing of the temple after its desecration by Antiochus Epiphanes, one of the cruelest rulers of all time.

A member of the Seleucid dynasty of Syria, Antiochus IV (175–164 B.C.) was surnamed Epiphanes, meaning "God manifest." His enemies, however, called him Epimanes, or "madman." Enterprising and ambitious, he desired to unify his empire by spreading Greek civilization and culture. This brought him into direct conflict with the Jews.

In a show of utter contempt for their religion, Antiochus erected an altar to the Greek god Zeus over the altar in the temple at Jerusalem. He also forced Jews to participate in heathen festivities and ordered them put to death if caught with the Law in their possession.

In 165 B.C., a man named Judas Maccabeus led a successful revolt that overthrew Seleucid domination of Palestine. The temple was cleansed on the 25th of Chislev, around December 25th by our calendar. Antiochus retreated to Persia, where, true to his nickname, he died a madman.

them. ⁹I am the door. If anyone enters by Me, he will be saved, and will go in and out and find pasture. ¹⁰The thief does not come except to steal, and to kill, and to destroy. I have come that they may have life, and that they may have *it* more abundantly.

¹¹"I am the good shepherd. The good shepherd gives His life for the sheep. ¹²But a hireling, *he who is* not the shepherd, one who does not own the sheep, sees the wolf coming and leaves the sheep and flees; and the wolf catches the sheep and scatters them. ¹³The hireling flees because he is a hireling and does not care about the sheep. ¹⁴I am the good shepherd; and I know My *sheep,* and am known by My own. ¹⁵As the Father knows Me, even so I know the Father; and I lay down My life for the sheep. ¹⁶And other sheep I have which are not of this fold; them also I must bring, and they will hear My voice; and there will be one flock *and* one shepherd.

10:17–18
see pg. 365

¹⁷"Therefore My Father loves Me, because I lay down My life that I may take it again. ¹⁸No one takes it from Me, but I lay it down of Myself. I have power to lay it down, and I have power to take it again. This command I have received from My Father."

¹⁹Therefore there was a division again among the Jews because of these sayings. ²⁰And many of them said, "He has a demon and is mad. Why do you listen to Him?"

²¹Others said, "These are not the words of one who has a demon. Can a demon open the eyes of the blind?"

Jesus Attends the Feast of Dedication

10:22

²²Now it was the Feast of Dedication in Jerusalem, and it was winter. ²³And Jesus walked in the temple, in Solomon's porch. ²⁴Then the Jews surrounded Him and said to Him, "How long do You keep us in doubt? If You are the Christ, tell us plainly."

²⁵Jesus answered them, "I told you, and you do not believe. The works that I do in My Father's name, they bear witness of Me. ²⁶But you do not believe, because you are not of My sheep, as I said to you.ᵃ ²⁷My sheep hear My voice, and I know them, and they follow Me. ²⁸And I give them eternal life, and they shall never perish; neither shall anyone snatch them out of My hand. ²⁹My Father, who has given *them* to Me, is greater than all; and no one is able to snatch *them* out of My Father's hand. ³⁰I and *My* Father are one."

10:31

³¹Then the Jews took up stones again to stone Him. ³²Jesus answered them, "Many good works I have shown you from My Father. For which of those works do you stone Me?"

10:26 ᵃNU-Text omits as I said to you.

33The Jews answered Him, saying, "For a good work we do not stone You, but for blasphemy, and because You, being a Man, make Yourself God."

34Jesus answered them, "Is it not written in your law, 'I said, "You are gods" '?*a* 35If He called them gods, to whom the word of God came (and the Scripture cannot be broken), 36do you say of Him whom the Father sanctified and sent into the world, 'You are blaspheming,' because I said, 'I am the Son of God'? 37If I do not do the works of My Father, do not believe Me; 38but if I do, though you do not believe Me, believe the works, that you may know and believe*a* that the Father *is* in Me, and I in Him." 39Therefore they sought again to seize Him, but He escaped out of their hand.

Jesus Returns to the River Jordan

10:40–42
see pg. 369

40And He went away again beyond the Jordan to the place where John was baptizing at first, and there He stayed. 41Then many came to Him and said, "John performed no sign, but all the things that John spoke about this Man were true." 42And many believed in Him there.

CHAPTER 11

Lazarus Raised from the Dead

11:1–2
see pg. 369

11:2
see pg. 370

1Now a certain *man* was sick, Lazarus of Bethany, the town of Mary and her sister Martha. 2It was *that* Mary who anointed the Lord with fragrant oil and wiped His feet with her hair, whose brother Lazarus was sick. 3Therefore the sisters sent to Him, saying, "Lord, behold, he whom You love is sick."

4When Jesus heard *that,* He said, "This sickness is not unto death, but for the glory of God, that the Son of God may be glorified through it."

5Now Jesus loved Martha and her sister and Lazarus. 6So, when He heard that he was sick, He stayed two more days in the place where He was. 7Then after this He said to *the* disciples, "Let us go to Judea again."

8*The* disciples said to Him, "Rabbi, lately the Jews sought to stone You, and are You going there again?"

9Jesus answered, "Are there not twelve hours in the day? If anyone walks in the day, he does not stumble, because he sees the light of this world. 10But if one walks in the night, he stumbles, because the light is not in him." 11These things

---

STONING

✓ FOR YOUR INFO
10:31

The intensity of the Jews' hostility against Jesus can be seen in their readiness to stone Him (v. 31; 8:59). Stoning was an ancient method of capital punishment reserved for the most serious crimes against the Mosaic Law, including:

- child sacrifice (Lev. 20:2).
- consultation with mediums and occultists (Lev. 20:27).
- blasphemy (Lev. 24:16).
- Sabbath-breaking (Num. 15:32–36).
- the worship of false gods (Deut. 13:10).
- rebellion against parents (Deut. 21:21).
- adultery (Ezek. 16:40).
- certain cases of direct disobedience against God's express command (Josh. 7:25).

Stoning was usually carried out by the men of the community (Deut. 21:21) upon the testimony of at least two witnesses, who were to cast the first stones (17:5–7). The execution usually took place outside the camp or city (Lev. 24:14, 23; 1 Kin. 21:10, 13).

Jesus must have known He was headed for trouble when His enemies "surrounded" Him (literally, "closed in on Him,") as He walked in Solomon's porch (vv. 23–24). In the same way, a victim of stoning would be surrounded as the executioners cut all means of escape from their fury.

BETHANY

Home of Mary, Martha, and Lazarus.

Jordan River

Jericho •
Bethabara •

Jerusalem •
Bethphage •
Qumran •

• Bethlehem

Dead Sea

0   3   6
Miles

N

BETHANY

YOU ARE THERE
11:18

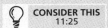

• **A village about two miles east of Jerusalem on the southeast slope of the Mount of Olives, on the road to Jericho.**
• **Name meant "house of an unripe fig," though its modern Arab**

(continued on next page)

John 11

He said, and after that He said to them, "Our friend Lazarus sleeps, but I go that I may wake him up."

[12]Then His disciples said, "Lord, if he sleeps he will get well." [13]However, Jesus spoke of his death, but they thought that He was speaking about taking rest in sleep.

[14]Then Jesus said to them plainly, "Lazarus is dead. [15]And

(Bible text continued on page 370)

PERSONALITY PROFILE: LAZARUS

☑ FOR YOUR INFO
11:1–45

Not to be confused with: The man named Lazarus in one of Jesus' parables (Luke 16:19–31).

Home: Bethany, near Jerusalem.

Family: Brother of Mary and Martha.

Occupation: Unknown.

Known today as: A man whom Jesus raised from the dead.

💡 CONSIDER THIS
11:25

"I AM THE RESURRECTION AND THE LIFE"

I t was after the raising of Lazarus from the dead that the chief priests, Pharisees, and other religious leaders finally determined to put Jesus to death (John 11:53). Until now, the conflict between them and the upstart rabbi had been little more than a war of words. But the raising of Lazarus was an incredible miracle, witnessed by many. Jesus had raised at least two others, but those events had taken place in faraway Galilee (Mark 5:22–24, 35–43; Luke 7:11–17). By contrast, Lazarus' resurrection occurred in Bethany, a suburb of Jerusalem (John 11:18).

Not surprisingly, the miracle caused many to believe in Jesus (v. 45). It provided undeniable proof that Jesus' bold claim must be true: "I am the resurrection and the life . . . and whoever lives and believes in Me shall never die" (v. 25). Indeed, Lazarus became something of a curiosity, drawing numerous onlookers who wanted to see for themselves the man whom Jesus had brought back to life (12:9).

It was this kind of publicity that the leaders especially feared. Disputes over religious matters were one thing; a rapidly growing movement led by a popular Messiah-

PERSONALITY PROFILE: MARY OF BETHANY

✓ **FOR YOUR INFO**
11:1–2

Not to be confused with: Mary, the mother of Jesus (Luke 1:26–56); Mary of Magdala (8:2); Mary, the mother of James and Joses (Matt. 27:55–61); Mary, the mother of John Mark (Acts 12:12).

Home: Bethany, a suburb of Jerusalem on the road to Jericho.

Family: Sister of Martha and Lazarus.

Best known today for: Sitting at Jesus' feet to worship and learn while her sister, Martha, served Him and His hungry disciples (Luke 10:38–42).

(continued from previous page)

name is el-'Azariyeh, "home of Lazarus."

- A favorite stopover for Jesus on His trips to and from Jerusalem. He stayed with His close friends Mary, Martha, and Lazarus.
- Modern Bethany offers a tomb site that some claim to be the authentic tomb of Lazarus, whom Jesus raised from the dead (John 11:1–44).

A nearby village, Bethphage ("place of young figs") along with Bethany may have given rise to Jesus' parable of the unripe figs (Luke 13:6–9). See "Bethphage," Mark 11:1.

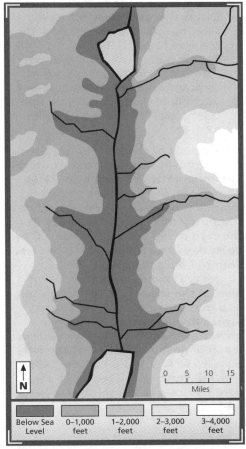

figure was something else. It was bound to have political repercussions, as the Romans were ever on the lookout for signs of rebellion (see "Jerusalem Surrounded," Luke 21:20).

It was Caiaphas the high priest (see Matt. 26:3) who saw the usefulness of that fact. Why sacrifice the entire nation for the sake of Jesus, when Jesus could be sacrificed for the sake of the nation (John 11:49–52)? Thus the religious leaders began to scheme how they might bring Jesus before the Romans and, hopefully, have Him put away on a charge of rebellion. And even though Lazarus had just been brought back from the dead, they plotted to do away with him as well, as he was living evidence of Jesus' power (12:10–11).

The plan succeeded brilliantly except for one detail that Caiaphas and his fellow leaders either overlooked or refused to believe: in arranging His death, they handed Him an opportunity to prove once and for all that He had spoken the truth when He said, "I am the resurrection and the life." ◆

| Below Sea Level | 0–1,000 feet | 1–2,000 feet | 2–3,000 feet | 3–4,000 feet |

 **YOU ARE THERE**
10:40–42

THE JORDAN RIVER VALLEY

THE DEVOTED MARY

💡 **CONSIDER THIS**
11:2 Scripture records only one sentence spoken by Mary of Bethany (John 11:32), and even that wasn't original: her sister Martha had already said the same thing (v. 21)! But what Mary may have lacked in outspokenness, she more than made up for in devotion to Jesus. All three portraits of her in the Gospels show her at the Lord's feet:

- **During one of Jesus' visits to her home, Mary sat at His feet, listening (Luke 10:38–42).**
- **When Jesus came to Bethany after Lazarus' death, Mary fell at His feet, completely broken over the tragedy (John 11:32).**
- **During a Passover meal just before Jesus' death, Mary poured fragrant oil on His head and feet, and wiped His feet with her hair (Matt. 26:6–13; Mark 14:3–9; John 12:1–8).**

On each of these occasions, this quiet woman was criticized by others. But apparently she didn't notice or didn't care. Mary seemed to be a woman who made choices based on a commitment to Jesus that went to the core of her being. In return, Jesus defended her actions, giving her freedom to be His disciple.

Mary is a model for anyone who lives in the shadow of a strong sibling or parent, or who prefers to listen rather than to speak. She demonstrates that preaching sermons or leading movements are not the only ways to follow Jesus. One can also show devotion by listening to the Lord's voice and worshiping at His feet.

Mary's sister, Martha, was an industrious, practical woman who never hesitated to speak her mind. Learn more about her at Luke 10:38–42.

I am glad for your sakes that I was not there, that you may believe. Nevertheless let us go to him."

16Then Thomas, who is called the Twin, said to his fellow disciples, "Let us also go, that we may die with Him."

17So when Jesus came, He found that he had already been 🌍 **11:18**
see pg. 368 in the tomb four days. 18Now Bethany was near Jerusalem, about two miles*a* away. 19And many of the Jews had joined the women around Martha and Mary, to comfort them concerning their brother.

20Now Martha, as soon as she heard that Jesus was coming, went and met Him, but Mary was sitting in the house. 21Now Martha said to Jesus, "Lord, if You had been here, my brother would not have died. 22But even now I know that whatever You ask of God, God will give You."

23Jesus said to her, "Your brother will rise again."

24Martha said to Him, "I know that he will rise again in the resurrection at the last day."

💡 **11:25**
see pg. 368 25Jesus said to her, "I am the resurrection and the life. He who believes in Me, though he may die, he shall live. 26And whoever lives and believes in Me shall never die. Do you believe this?"

27She said to Him, "Yes, Lord, I believe that You are the Christ, the Son of God, who is to come into the world."

28And when she had said these things, she went her way and secretly called Mary her sister, saying, "The Teacher has come and is calling for you." 29As soon as she heard *that,* she arose quickly and came to Him. 30Now Jesus had not yet come into the town, but was*a* in the place where Martha met Him. 31Then the Jews who were with her in the house, and comforting her, when they saw that Mary rose up quickly and went out, followed her, saying, "She is going to the tomb to weep there."*a*

32Then, when Mary came where Jesus was, and saw Him, she fell down at His feet, saying to Him, "Lord, if You had been here, my brother would not have died."

33Therefore, when Jesus saw her weeping, and the Jews who came with her weeping, He groaned in the spirit and was troubled. 34And He said, "Where have you laid him?"

They said to Him, "Lord, come and see."

35Jesus wept. 36Then the Jews said, "See how He loved him!"

37And some of them said, "Could not this Man, who opened the eyes of the blind, also have kept this man from dying?"

38Then Jesus, again groaning in Himself, came to the

11:18 aLiterally fifteen stadia   11:30 aNU-Text adds still.   11:31 aNU-Text reads supposing that she was going to the tomb to weep there.

tomb. It was a cave, and a stone lay against it. ³⁹Jesus said, "Take away the stone."

Martha, the sister of him who was dead, said to Him, "Lord, by this time there is a stench, for he has been *dead* four days."

⁴⁰Jesus said to her, "Did I not say to you that if you would

11:17–45
see pg. 372

believe you would see the glory of God?" ⁴¹Then they took away the stone *from the place* where the dead man was lying.ᵃ And Jesus lifted up *His* eyes and said, "Father, I thank You that You have heard Me. ⁴²And I know that You always hear Me, but because of the people who are standing by I said *this,* that they may be-

11:1–45
see pg. 368

lieve that You sent Me." ⁴³Now when He had said these things, He cried with a loud voice, "Lazarus, come forth!" ⁴⁴And he who had died came out bound hand and foot with graveclothes, and his face was wrapped with a cloth. Jesus said to them, "Loose him, and let him go."

Leaders Plot to Destroy Jesus

⁴⁵Then many of the Jews who had come to Mary, and had seen the things Jesus did, believed in Him. ⁴⁶But some of them went away to the Pharisees and told them the things Jesus did. ⁴⁷Then the chief priests and the Pharisees gathered a council and said, "What shall we do? For this Man works many signs. ⁴⁸If we let Him alone like this, everyone will believe in Him, and the Romans will come and take away both our place and nation."

11:49

⁴⁹And one of them, Caiaphas, being high priest that year, said to them, "You know nothing at all, ⁵⁰nor do you consider that it is expedient for usᵃ that one man should die for the people, and not that the whole nation should perish." ⁵¹Now this he did not say on his own *authority;* but being high priest that year he prophesied that Jesus would die for the nation, ⁵²and not for that nation only, but also that He would gather together in one the children of God who were scattered abroad.

⁵³Then, from that day on, they plotted to put Him to

11:54

death. ⁵⁴Therefore Jesus no longer walked openly among the Jews, but went from there into the country near the wilderness, to a city called Ephraim, and there remained with His disciples.

11:41 ᵃNU-Text omits *from the place where the dead man was lying.*   11:50 ᵃNU-Text reads *you.*

❖ ❖

Caiaphas

A CLOSER LOOK
11:49

Troubled by the confusion created by the raising of Lazarus, Caiaphas, the high priest, scorned his fellow leaders as know-nothings (v. 49). But what do we know about the man Caiaphas? See Matt. 26:3.

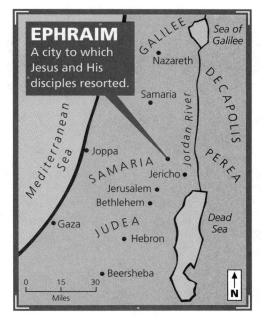

EPHRAIM

YOU ARE THERE
11:54

• A city surrounded by mountains, four miles east of Bethel and fourteen miles northeast of Jerusalem.

• Also known as Ephron and Ephrain. Ephraim was of one of the twelve tribes of Israel.

• Name meant "doubly fruitful" or "double grain land."

• Identified with the Old Testament city of Ophrah (Josh. 18:23; 1 Sam. 13:17), at site of modern et-Taiyibeh.

JESUS RAISES LAZARUS

💡 **CONSIDER THIS**
11:17–45

The final sign miracle in John's Gospel is the climax of Jesus' signs: He raised Lazarus from the dead (vv. 41–44), proving to all that He was master even over death. The amazing thing was that this miracle led directly to the plot to arrest Him and put Him to death (vv. 46–53), along with Lazarus (12:10–11)!

⁵⁵And the Passover of the Jews was near, and many went from the country up to Jerusalem before the Passover, to purify themselves. ⁵⁶Then they sought Jesus, and spoke among themselves as they stood in the temple, "What do you think—that He will not come to the feast?" ⁵⁷Now both the chief priests and the Pharisees had given a command, that if anyone knew where He was, he should report *it*, that they might seize Him.

CHAPTER 12

Mary Anoints Jesus with Costly Oil

 12:1–8

¹Then, six days before the Passover, Jesus came to Bethany, where Lazarus was who had been dead,ᵃ whom He had raised from the dead. ²There they made Him a supper; and Martha served, but Lazarus was one of those who sat at the table with Him. ³Then Mary took a pound of very costly oil of spikenard, anointed the feet of Jesus, and wiped His feet with her hair. And the house was filled with the fragrance of the oil.

12:1 ᵃNU-Text omits *who had been dead.*

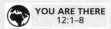 **YOU ARE THERE**
12:1–8

FUNERAL PREPARATIONS

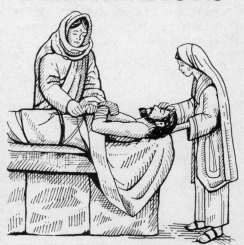

Jesus told the dinner crowd that Mary was preparing Him for His burial (v. 7). It's difficult for us today to appreciate the significance that burial rituals had for ancient peoples. Nearly every ancient religion gave explicit and sometimes elaborate instructions for preparing and burying the dead.

For Hebrews at the time of Christ, women and men participated in the mourning ritual, but women likely prepared the corpse for interment. First they washed the body, then scented it with fragrant oil, an act of devotion that might be repeated at the tomb.

The oil that Mary used on Jesus (v. 3) was probably nard, a perfume used by women. Imported from India, it was extremely costly and was known for its strong fragrance. It was the same perfume used by the woman that Solomon praised in his Song of Solomon (1:12; 4:13).

Washed and scented, the body was dressed in the person's own clothes or else wrapped in specially prepared sheets. Then, as soon as possible, it was carried upon a bier to the tomb. Relatives, friends, and professional mourners (see Matt. 9:23) formed a procession, and anyone meeting it was obliged to show honor to the

🔍 **12:4–7** ⁴But one of His disciples, Judas Iscariot, Simon's *son,* who would betray Him, said, ⁵"Why was this fragrant oil not sold for three hundred denariiᵃ and given to the poor?" ⁶This he said, not that he cared for the poor, but because he was a thief, and had the money box; and he used to take what was put in it.

⁷But Jesus said, "Let her alone; she has keptᵃ this for the day of My burial. ⁸For the poor you have with you always, but Me you do not have always."

The Curious Gather

⁹Now a great many of the Jews knew that He was there; and they came, not for Jesus' sake only, but that they might also see Lazarus, whom He had raised from the dead. ¹⁰But the chief priests plotted to put Lazarus to death also, ¹¹because on account of him many of the Jews went away and believed in Jesus.

12:5 ᵃAbout one year's wages for a worker   12:7 ᵃNU-Text reads *that she may keep.*

Why Not Give to the Poor?

🔍 **A CLOSER LOOK 12:4–7** *Judas Iscariot's greedy heart was clearly revealed in this incident (vv. 4–6). But Jesus responded with a puzzling statement (vv. 7–8). For an explanation, see "A Parting Gift," Mark 14:3–9.*

deceased and the relatives by joining. A eulogy was often delivered at the grave site.

The body was placed on a shelf in the tomb, which was then sealed by a heavy, tight-fitting slab. Jews were expected to visit the tomb often, partly as a precaution against burying someone who only seemed dead. ◆

For further details see "Burial" at 1 Cor. 15:42.

> "**F**OR THE POOR YOU HAVE WITH YOU ALWAYS, BUT **M**E YOU DO NOT HAVE ALWAYS."
> —John 12:8

A Parade Welcomes Jesus to Jerusalem

[12]The next day a great multitude that had come to the feast, when they heard that Jesus was coming to Jerusalem, [13]took branches of palm trees and went out to meet Him, and cried out:

> "Hosanna!
> 'Blessed is He who comes in the name of the LORD!'[a]
> The King of Israel!"

[14]Then Jesus, when He had found a young donkey, sat on it; as it is written:

> [15] "Fear not, daughter of Zion;
> Behold, your King is coming,
> Sitting on a donkey's colt."[a]

[16]His disciples did not understand these things at first; but when Jesus was glorified, then they remembered that these things were written about Him and that they had done these things to Him. [17]Therefore the people, who were with Him when He called Lazarus out of his tomb and raised him from the dead, bore witness. [18]For this reason the people also met Him, because they heard that He had done this sign. [19]The Pharisees therefore said among themselves, "You see that you are accomplishing nothing. Look, the world has gone after Him!"

Jesus Sums Up His Teaching

12:20–36 [20]Now there were certain Greeks among those who came up to worship at the feast. [21]Then they came to Philip, who was from Bethsaida of Galilee, and asked him, saying, "Sir, we wish to see Jesus."

[22]Philip came and told Andrew, and in turn Andrew and Philip told Jesus.

[23]But Jesus answered them, saying, "The hour has come that the Son of Man should be glorified. [24]Most assuredly, I say to you, unless a grain of wheat falls into the ground and dies, it remains alone; but if it dies, it produces much grain. [25]He who loves his life will lose it, and he who hates his life in this world will keep it for eternal life. [26]If anyone serves Me, let him follow Me; and where I am, there My servant will be also. If anyone serves Me, him My Father will honor.

[27]"Now My soul is troubled, and what shall I say? 'Father, save Me from this hour'? But for this purpose I came to this hour. [28]Father, glorify Your name."

12:13 [a]Psalm 118:26   12:15 [a]Zechariah 9:9

JESUS EXCLUDES ONLY THE FAITHLESS

CONSIDER THIS 12:20–36 Jesus was at an annual Jewish festival called Passover (12:1). It was a major feast, lasting several days and attended by people from all over the Roman Empire (see Luke 22:7).

When Gentiles at the Passover requested a meeting with Jesus, He responded by telling His Jewish followers that He was going to draw all peoples to Himself (v. 32). Later He affirmed that nothing can save someone from judgment but faith in Him and His saving work on the cross (vv. 46, 48). Nothing else helps, nor does the lack of any other qualification prohibit anyone from coming to Jesus for salvation.

Then a voice came from heaven, *saying,* "I have both glorified *it* and will glorify *it* again."

²⁹Therefore the people who stood by and heard *it* said that it had thundered. Others said, "An angel has spoken to Him."

³⁰Jesus answered and said, "This voice did not come because of Me, but for your sake. ³¹Now is the judgment of this world; now the ruler of this world will be cast out. ³²And I, if I am lifted up from the earth, will draw all *peoples* to Myself." ³³This He said, signifying by what death He would die.

³⁴The people answered Him, "We have heard from the law that the Christ remains forever; and how *can* You say, 'The Son of Man must be lifted up'? Who is this Son of Man?"

³⁵Then Jesus said to them, "A little while longer the light is with you. Walk while you have the light, lest darkness overtake you; he who walks in darkness does not know where he is going. ³⁶While you have the light, believe in the light, that you may become sons of light." These things Jesus spoke, and departed, and was hidden from them.

Unbelief Persists

³⁷But although He had done so many signs before them, they did not believe in Him, ³⁸that the word of Isaiah the prophet might be fulfilled, which he spoke:

"Lord, who has believed our report?
And to whom has the arm of the LORD been revealed?"ᵃ

³⁹Therefore they could not believe, because Isaiah said again:

40 "He has blinded their eyes and hardened their hearts,
Lest they should see with *their* eyes,
Lest they should understand with *their* hearts and turn,
So that I should heal them." ᵃ

⁴¹These things Isaiah said whenᵃ he saw His glory and spoke of Him.

⁴²Nevertheless even among the rulers many believed in Him, but because of the Pharisees they did not confess *Him,* lest they should be put out of the synagogue; ⁴³for they loved the praise of men more than the praise of God.

Jesus Makes His Final Claims

⁴⁴Then Jesus cried out and said, "He who believes in Me, believes not in Me but in Him who sent Me. ⁴⁵And he who

12:38 ᵃIsaiah 53:1   12:40 ᵃIsaiah 6:10   12:41 ᵃNU-Text reads *because.*

THE FEAR OF REJECTION

CONSIDER THIS
12:42–43

As John points out in vv. 42–43, the Pharisees held a powerful grip on Jewish society in Jesus' day, stifling dissent through fear. Apparently Jesus had some support even at the highest levels of society. But it did Him no good, as fear of rejection overcame the impulse for justice and truth.

Have you ever been embarrassed or afraid to identify publicly with Christ because of possible rejection by others, especially superiors? Scripture is clear that one price of authentic discipleship will almost certainly be some rejection and persecution (15:18–25; 2 Tim. 3:12). To believe that you can avoid any tough choices between acceptance by the world and loyalty to God is both naive and dangerous. If God does not hold your highest allegiance, how real can He be to you in any meaningful way?

The Pharisees were one of a number of major political parties among the Hebrews in the first century. See "Party Politics of Jesus' Day," Matt. 16:1.

THE ORDER OF THE TOWEL

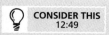
CONSIDER THIS
13:1–20
Leadership is a fascinating topic. Business books offer models of leadership as diverse as Attila the Hun, Oriental warlords, and Abraham Lincoln. But Jesus painted a different picture of leadership.

As He wrapped up His work, Jesus held a dinner for His closest associates. Instead of delivering a state-of-the-union address or naming a successor, He chose to leave His seat at the head of the table and pick up some household servant's equipment—a basin of water and a towel. He then washed the feet of every person at the table—even Judas, His betrayer (vv. 1–20). Foot-washing was usually performed by household servants as an act of hospitality to weary, dusty guests (compare Luke 7:44). Leaders and hosts did not stoop to such a menial task. But Jesus did.

(continued on next page)

John 12, 13

sees Me sees Him who sent Me. [46]I have come *as* a light into the world, that whoever believes in Me should not abide in darkness. [47]And if anyone hears My words and does not believe,[a] I do not judge him; for I did not come to judge the world but to save the world. [48]He who rejects Me, and does not receive My words, has that which judges him—the

CONSIDER THIS 12:49

word that I have spoken will judge him in the last day. [49]For I have not spoken on My own *authority;* but the Father who sent Me gave Me a command, what I should say and what I should speak. [50]And I know that His command is everlasting life. Therefore, whatever I speak, just as the Father has told Me, so I speak."

CHAPTER 13

Jesus Washes the Disciples' Feet

CONSIDER THIS 13:1–20

[1]Now before the Feast of the Passover, when Jesus knew that His hour had come that He should depart from this world to the Father, having loved His own who were in the world, He loved them to the end.

CONSIDER THIS 13:2–17

[2]And supper being ended,[a] the devil having already put it into the heart of Judas Iscariot, Simon's *son,* to betray Him, [3]Jesus, knowing

12:47 [a]NU-Text reads *keep them.* 13:2 [a]NU-Text reads *And during supper.*

CONSIDER THIS
12:49

UNDER AUTHORITY

Jesus faithfully represented His Father to the world (v. 49). Consider two implications of that for Christians today:

(1) As believers, we are to live under Christ's authority, and therefore we are responsible for faithfully representing Christ in our places of work. To do so we must be intimately familiar with Jesus—what He said, what His commands are, and what His purposes are. That means serious and continuous exploration of the Scriptures.

(2) As employees under human authorities, we are responsible for faithfully representing our organizations in general and our superiors in particular to other people. To do so we must be intimately familiar with the values, goals, policies, and procedures of our employers.

Neither of these is an easy assignment. It's all too common to misrepresent the statements of the Lord or our superiors to suit our own purposes. It's also easy to hear from them only what we want to hear.

that the Father had given all things into His hands, and that He had come from God and was going to God, [4]rose from supper and laid aside His garments, took a towel and girded Himself. [5]After that, He poured water into a basin and began to wash the disciples' feet, and to wipe *them* with the towel with which He was girded. [6]Then He came to Simon Peter. And *Peter* said to Him, "Lord, are You washing my feet?"

[7]Jesus answered and said to him, "What I am doing you do not understand now, but you will know after this."

[8]Peter said to Him, "You shall never wash my feet!"

Jesus answered him, "If I do not wash you, you have no part with Me."

[9]Simon Peter said to Him, "Lord, not my feet only, but also *my* hands and *my* head!"

[10]Jesus said to him, "He who is bathed needs only to wash *his* feet, but is completely clean; and you are clean, but not all of you." [11]For He knew who would betray Him; therefore He said, "You are not all clean."

[12]So when He had washed their feet, taken His garments, and sat down again, He said to them, "Do you know what I have done to you? [13]You call Me Teacher and Lord, and you say well, for *so* I am. [14]If I then, *your* Lord and Teacher, have washed your feet, you also ought to wash one another's feet. [15]For I have given you an example, that you should do as I have done to you. [16]Most assuredly, I say to you, a servant is not greater than his master; nor is he who is sent greater

• • • • • • • • • • • • • • • • • • • •

Are there any checks and balances to guard against those temptations? Jesus modeled two principles for us. First, He asked questions and listened to answers: for example, with Nicodemus (3:1–21) and with the woman at the well (4:1–26). Furthermore, He was clear about His mission and secure in His position. As a result, He never felt compelled to prove or promote Himself. In this He differed from many of the leaders of His day, who "loved the praise of men more than the praise of God" (12:43). ◆

Scripture has much more to say about our relationship to our employers. See "Who's the Boss?" Col. 3:22–24.

(continued from previous page)

Seated once again at the table, the Lord asked whether His followers understood what He had done (John 13:12). He then exhorted them to adopt the same posture of serving others, thereby following His example. He assured them that they would be blessed if they did (vv. 15–17).

Jesus still calls believers today to become members of the "Order of the Towel." As Christ's followers, we need to lead others by serving them.

In a related incident, Jesus spelled out what servant-leadership means. See "Servant-Leaders," Matt. 20:25–28.

A MODEL OF SERVANT-LEADERSHIP

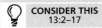 **CONSIDER THIS 13:2–17** *When Jesus washed His disciples' feet (vv. 3–5), He demonstrated a fundamental principle that He regularly stressed to His followers: To lead others, one must serve others. This is as true in public life and the business world as it is in the church. No number of corporate memos or rah-rah speeches exhorting workers to commit themselves to an organization or its clients will have as powerful an impact as a person of authority modeling consistently and clearly the attitude of a servant: placing others' needs before one's own, committing oneself to doing concrete things to meet those needs, and looking for neither favors nor reciprocity from the people one serves.*

THE HALLMARK OF LOVE

CONSIDER THIS
13:31–35

A key test of our commitment to Christ is our love for other believers (vv. 31–35). It is not just our words that express our love, but our attitudes and actions as well. Jesus did not say that others would know we are His disciples by what we say, or how we dress, or what we know, or the label of our denomination. He said, "as I have loved you" (v. 34). Shortly afterward, He laid down His life for those first believers.

" . . . **H**AVE
LOVE
FOR
ONE
ANOTHER."
—John 13:35

than he who sent him. ¹⁷If you know these things, blessed are you if you do them.

¹⁸"I do not speak concerning all of you. I know whom I have chosen; but that the Scripture may be fulfilled, 'He who eats bread with Me*a* has lifted up his heel against Me.'*b* ¹⁹Now I tell you before it comes, that when it does come to pass, you may believe that I am *He*. ²⁰Most assuredly, I say to you, he who receives whomever I send receives Me; and he who receives Me receives Him who sent Me."

Judas Leaves to Betray Jesus

²¹When Jesus had said these things, He was troubled in spirit, and testified and said, "Most assuredly, I say to you, one of you will betray Me." ²²Then the disciples looked at one another, perplexed about whom He spoke.

²³Now there was leaning on Jesus' bosom one of His disciples, whom Jesus loved. ²⁴Simon Peter therefore motioned to him to ask who it was of whom He spoke.

²⁵Then, leaning back*a* on Jesus' breast, he said to Him, "Lord, who is it?"

²⁶Jesus answered, "It is he to whom I shall give a piece of bread when I have dipped *it*." And having dipped the bread, He gave *it* to Judas Iscariot, *the son* of Simon. ²⁷Now after the piece of bread, Satan entered him. Then Jesus said to him, "What you do, do quickly." ²⁸But no one at the table knew for what reason He said this to him. ²⁹For some thought, because Judas had the money box, that Jesus had said to him, "Buy *those things* we need for the feast," or that he should give something to the poor.

³⁰Having received the piece of bread, he then went out immediately. And it was night.

A New Commandment

13:31–35

³¹So, when he had gone out, Jesus said, "Now the Son of Man is glorified, and God is glorified in Him. ³²If God is glorified in Him, God will also glorify Him in Himself, and glorify Him immediately. ³³Little children, I shall be with you a little while longer. You will seek Me; and as I said to the Jews, 'Where I am going, you cannot come,' so now I say to you. ³⁴A new commandment I give to you, that you love one another; as I have loved you, that you also love one another. ³⁵By this all will know that you are My disciples, if you have love for one another."

Jesus Predicts Peter's Denial

³⁶Simon Peter said to Him, "Lord, where are You going?" Jesus answered him, "Where I am going you cannot

13:18 *a*NU-Text reads *My bread.*   *b*Psalm 41:9   13:25 *a*NU-Text and M-Text add *thus.*

follow Me now, but you shall follow Me afterward."

³⁷Peter said to Him, "Lord, why can I not follow You now? I will lay down my life for Your sake."

³⁸Jesus answered him, "Will you lay down your life for My sake? Most assuredly, I say to you, the rooster shall not crow till you have denied Me three times.

CHAPTER 14

"I Am the Way, the Truth, and the Life"

¹"Let not your heart be troubled; you believe in God, believe also in Me. ²In My Father's house are many mansions;ᵃ if *it were* not *so,* I would have told you. I go to prepare a place for you.ᵇ ³And if I go and prepare a place for you, I will come again and receive you to Myself; that where I am, *there* you may be also. ⁴And where I go you know, and the way you know."

⁵Thomas said to Him, "Lord, we do not know where You are going, and how can we know the way?"

⁶Jesus said to him, "I am the way, the truth, and the life. No one comes to the Father except through Me.

⁷"If you had known Me, you would have known My Father also; and from now on you know Him and have seen Him."

⁸Philip said to Him, "Lord, show us the Father, and it is sufficient for us."

⁹Jesus said to him, "Have I been with you so long, and yet you have not known Me, Philip? He who has seen Me has seen the Father; so how can you say, 'Show us the Father'? ¹⁰Do you not believe that I am in the Father, and the Father in Me? The words that I speak to you I do not speak on My own *authority;* but the Father who dwells in Me does the works. ¹¹Believe Me that I *am* in the Father and the Father in Me, or else believe Me for the sake of the works themselves.

14:12–13

¹²"Most assuredly, I say to you, he who believes in Me, the works that I do he will do also; and greater *works* than these he will do, because I go to My Father. ¹³And whatever you ask in My name, that I will do, that the Father may be glorified in the Son. ¹⁴If you askᵃ anything in My name, I will do *it.*

The Holy Spirit Is Promised

14:16–18

¹⁵"If you love Me, keepᵃ My commandments. ¹⁶And I will pray the Father, and He will give you another Helper, that He may abide with

14:2 ᵃLiterally *dwellings* ᵇNU-Text adds a word which would cause the text to read either *if it were not so, would I have told you that I go to prepare a place for you?* or *if it were not so I would have told you; for I go to prepare a place for you.* 14:14 ᵃNU-Text adds *Me.* 14:15 ᵃNU-Text reads *you will keep.*

PEACE IN THE CHAOS

We live in a turbulent world. Change is rapid and frequently dramatic. Jesus said that He alone can provide the help and peace we need to live and work with integrity and wholeness (vv. 25–28). Certainly our work cannot be depended on for that. No job is engaging enough, no position powerful enough, and no material rewards substantial enough to give us the kind of inner peace and confidence we long for. Only Christ will never leave us nor forsake us.

you forever— [17]the Spirit of truth, whom the world cannot receive, because it neither sees Him nor knows Him; but you know Him, for He dwells with you and will be in you. [18]I will not leave you orphans; I will come to you.

[19]"A little while longer and the world will see Me no more, but you will see Me. Because I live, you will live also. [20]At that day you will know that I *am* in My Father, and you in Me, and I in you. [21]He who has My commandments and keeps them, it is he who loves Me. And he who loves Me will be loved by My Father, and I will love him and manifest Myself to him."

[22]Judas (not Iscariot) said to Him, "Lord, how is it that You will manifest Yourself to us, and not to the world?"

[23]Jesus answered and said to him, "If anyone loves Me, he will keep My word; and My Father will love him, and We will come to him and make Our home with him. [24]He who does not love Me does not keep My words; and the word which you hear is not Mine but the Father's who sent Me.

[25]"These things I have spoken to you while being present with you. [26]But the Helper, the Holy Spirit, whom the Father will send in My name, He will teach you all things, and bring to your remembrance all things that I said to you. [27]Peace I leave with

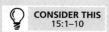
THE NETWORK

*C*omputer networks have become important systems in today's competitive marketplace. They enable teams of workers in different offices, at regional sites, and even from around the world to join together on tasks that would otherwise be difficult if not impossible.

One way of setting up a network is to use a central computer to handle the main programming, storage, and communication functions, with remote workstations for individual input and retrieval. This is similar to the situation that Jesus described in His image of the vine and the branches (vv. 1–10):

(1) Jesus is the key (v. 1). Like the central processing unit of a computer system, Jesus provides the life, the direction, and the commands for His followers, those of us "on-line."

(2) To be effective, believers must maintain their relationship with Jesus (v. 4). In order to use the features of a network, a user must remain attached to the network. If one "signs off," there is no more access to the central computer or to others in the network. Likewise, if we allow sin to disrupt our walk with Christ, we lose fellowship with Him and with other believers (1 John 1:6–7).

you, My peace I give to you; not as the world gives do I give to you. Let not your heart be troubled, neither let it be afraid. ²⁸You have heard Me say to you, 'I am going away and coming *back* to you.' If you loved Me, you would rejoice because I said,ª 'I am going to the Father,' for My Father is greater than I.

²⁹"And now I have told you before it comes, that when it does come to pass, you may believe. ³⁰I will no longer talk much with you, for the ruler of this world is coming, and he has nothing in Me. ³¹But that the world may know that I love the Father, and as the Father gave Me commandment, so I do. Arise, let us go from here.

CHAPTER 15

"I Am the Vine"

15:1–10 ¹"I am the true vine, and My Father is the vinedresser. ²Every branch in Me that does not bear fruit He takes away;ª and every *branch* that bears fruit He prunes, that it may bear more fruit. ³You are already clean because of the word which I have spoken to

14:28 ªNU-Text omits *I said.*   15:2 ªOr *lifts up*

(3) Jesus wants His followers to be productive (vv. 5–8). *Companies install computer networks so that their employees can get their work done. The systems cost too much to be treated as toys or to be underutilized. Correspondingly, the relationship that believers have with God was purchased through Christ's blood, so we need to take it seriously. Christ wants us to enjoy walking with Him, but He also wants us to accomplish His purposes.*
(4) To love Jesus is to follow His commands (vv. 9–10). *Occasionally network users receive an "error message" indicating that they have not followed the instructions of the program correctly. By the same token, Jesus has given us commands to follow, and the only way to experience His life and power is to obey those commands. To do so is not only practical, but an expression of our love for the Lord.*

Are you "on-line" with Jesus, drawing on His resources and obeying His commands? Is your life productive, accomplishing the tasks and responsibilities that He has assigned to you? ◆

"**E**VERY BRANCH THAT BEARS FRUIT **H**E PRUNES, THAT IT MAY BEAR MORE FRUIT."
—John 15:2

QUOTE UNQUOTE

CONSIDER THIS 15:18–20 *Just as the world rejected Jesus, it will reject His followers (vv. 18–20). One writer offers a few reasons why:*

A real Christian is an odd number anyway. He feels supreme love for One whom he has never seen; talks familiarly every day to Someone he cannot see; expects to go to heaven on the virtue of Another; empties himself in order to be full; admits he is wrong so he can be declared right; goes down in order to get up; is strongest when he is weakest; richest when he is poorest; and happiest when he feels the worst. He dies so he can live; forsakes in order to have; gives away so he can keep; sees the invisible; hears the inaudible; and knows that which passeth knowledge.

A. W. Tozer

you. ⁴Abide in Me, and I in you. As the branch cannot bear fruit of itself, unless it abides in the vine, neither can you, unless you abide in Me.

⁵"I am the vine, you *are* the branches. He who abides in Me, and I in him, bears much fruit; for without Me you can do nothing. ⁶If anyone does not abide in Me, he is cast out as a branch and is withered; and they gather them and throw *them* into the fire, and they are burned. ⁷If you abide in Me, and My words abide in you, you willᵃ ask what you desire, and it shall be done for you. ⁸By this My Father is glorified, that you bear much fruit; so you will be My disciples.

⁹"As the Father loved Me, I also have loved you; abide in My love. ¹⁰If you keep My commandments, you will abide in My love, just as I have kept My Father's commandments and abide in His love.

"Love One Another"

¹¹"These things I have spoken to you, that My joy may remain in you, and *that* your joy may be full. ¹²This is My commandment, that you love one another as I have loved you. ¹³Greater love has no one than this, than to lay down one's life for his friends. ¹⁴You are My friends if you do whatever I command you. ¹⁵No longer do I call you servants, for a servant does not know what his master is doing; but I have called you friends, for all things that I heard from My Father I have made known to you. ¹⁶You did not choose Me, but I chose you and appointed you that you should go and bear fruit, and *that* your fruit should remain, that whatever you ask the Father in My name He may give you. ¹⁷These things I command you, that you love one another.

15:18–20

15:18–25

¹⁸"If the world hates you, you know that it hated Me before *it hated* you. ¹⁹If you were of the world, the world would love its own. Yet because you are not of the world, but I chose you out of the world, therefore the world hates you. ²⁰Remember the word that I said to you, 'A servant is not greater than his master.' If they persecuted Me, they will also persecute you. If they kept My word, they will keep yours also. ²¹But all these things they will do to you for My name's sake, because they do not know Him who sent Me. ²²If I had not come and spoken to them, they would have no sin, but now they have no excuse for their sin. ²³He who hates Me hates My Father also. ²⁴If I had not done among them the works which no one else did, they would have no sin; but now they have seen and also hated both Me and My Father. ²⁵But *this happened* that the word

15:7 ᵃNU-Text omits *you will.*

might be fulfilled which is written in their law, 'They hated Me without a cause.'[a]

26"But when the Helper comes, whom I shall send to you from the Father, the Spirit of truth who proceeds from the Father, He will testify of Me. 27And you also will bear witness, because you have been with Me from the beginning.

CHAPTER 16

The Work of the Spirit

1"These things I have spoken to you, that you should not be made to stumble. 2They will put you out of the synagogues; yes, the time is coming that whoever kills you will think that he offers God service. 3And these things they will do to you[a] because they have not known the Father nor Me. 4But these things I have told you, that when the[a] time comes, you may remember that I told you of them.

"And these things I did not say to you at the beginning, because I was with you.

5"But now I go away to Him who sent Me, and none of you asks Me, 'Where are You going?' 6But because I have said these things to you, sorrow has filled your heart. 7Nevertheless I tell you the truth. It is to your advantage that I go away; for if I do not go away, the Helper will not come to you; but if I depart, I will send Him to you. 8And when He has come, He will convict the world of sin, and of righteousness, and of judgment: 9of sin, because they do not believe in Me; 10of righteousness, because I go to My Father and you see Me no more; 11of judgment, because the ruler of this world is judged.

12"I still have many things to say to you, but you cannot bear *them* now. 13However, when He, the Spirit of truth, has come, He will guide you into all truth; for He will not speak on His own *authority,* but whatever He hears He will speak; and He will tell you things to come. 14He will glorify Me, for He will take of what is Mine and declare *it* to you. 15All things that the Father has are Mine. Therefore I said that He will take of Mine and declare *it* to you.[a]

Temporary Sorrow, Then Permanent Joy

16"A little while, and you will not see Me; and again a little while, and you will see Me, because I go to the Father."

(Bible text continued on page 386)

15:25 [a]Psalm 69:4   16:3 [a]NU-Text and M-Text omit *to you.*   16:4 [a]NU-Text reads *their.*
16:15 [a]NU-Text and M-Text read *He takes of Mine and will declare it to you.*

THE COST OF FOLLOWING JESUS

CONSIDER THIS 15:18–25 **Are you prepared to be *hated* because of your commitment to Jesus Christ? Perhaps you expect to be misunderstood occasionally or even chided by associates for "going overboard" on religion. But Jesus used strong words in vv. 18–25: "hate" and "persecute." He indicated that our true commitments will be made clear when they start to cost us something.**

What has your faith cost you? A promotion or some other career opportunity? Criticism or even ostracism by coworkers or family? Legal action? Or nothing at all? Sooner or later, following Christ has a cost, and those who think they can get by without paying it are misguided. In fact, if there's no cost, is there really any genuine commitment? Jesus' words suggest not.

However, it's also possible for our actions or words to cause offense because they are inappropriate. In that case, the hostility we may receive is not persecution. Like Jesus (1:14), we are called to be people of grace and truth, not obnoxious and rude. True persecution involves unmerited hostility for doing good works in the pattern of Christ (1 Pet. 2:12–21).

Fear of rejection is one of the main reasons believers hesitate to declare their true colors. See John 12:42–43.

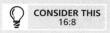
WHOSE JOB IS EVANGELISM?

One thing is certain about evangelism: both non-Christians and Christians feel uncomfortable with it. Bring up the topic of religion (let alone the gospel) with your unbelieving workmates, and the atmosphere suddenly tenses up. It's as if spiritual matters are out of place in a professional setting.

Consequently, many Christians fold their hands and shut their mouths when it comes to evangelism. They've decided it's up to God to bring people to faith. But they're not going to participate in the process.

Of course, in a way it is up to God to bring about salvation, as v. 8 shows. The Holy Spirit is *the* great evangelist. Yet other passages urge us as believers to work *with* the Spirit in influencing others with the gospel. To understand our role in this joint venture, we need to rediscover the evangelistic work of the Spirit. This involves:

Common grace. No matter how bad things get in the world—plagued as it is with war, poverty, famine, disease, crime, family chaos, and so on—things would be far worse if it weren't for God's Spirit. The Spirit moves throughout the world, restraining the full onslaught of evil and promoting whatever is good. The Spirit does this for believers and unbelievers alike; hence the name, "common grace."

Because of this gracious work, the unbeliever is in a position to accept God's offer of salvation, and therefore benefits from divine grace whether salvation occurs or not (Ps. 104:24–30).

Spiritual awakening. Unaware that God restrains evil and promotes good, an unbeliever can be glib about life and unapproachable concerning spiritual issues. So the Spirit's job is to awaken the unbeliever to his or her true spiritual condition. The Spirit may use a disturbing conscience, a declining hope, or a gripping fear. Other instruments include the law, government, and human kindness (Is. 57:20–21; Joel 2:28–32; Rom. 2:1–6, 15–16).

Conviction of sin. When the Spirit pricks an unbeliever's conscience, there may be feelings of acute guilt and fear of God's judgment (John 16:8; Acts 5:1–11). Such a person can become quite hostile, and even attack nearby believers. This is important to know; rejection of the gospel does not necessarily reflect failure on our part as Christ's representatives (though anger is justifiable if we're insensitive in our approach).

Regeneration. This part of evangelism is one that Christians too often take credit for, even though it is the work of the Spirit. Regeneration involves the giving of new life to a lost sinner (John 3:5–8). Only the Spirit can do that. As believers, we can do nothing but help this birthing process along.

Sealing and equipping. Finally, the Spirit "seals" the new believer in Christ; that is, the Spirit confirms and guarantees the believer's place in God's family and provides assurance of salvation (2 Cor. 5:5; Eph. 1:13). Moreover, the Spirit equips the new Christian to live and act as Christ's follower by providing spiritual power and gifts, and bonding believers together. New appetites develop—a love for Scripture, a hatred of evil, and a desire to share the faith.

In light of these evangelistic efforts of God's Spirit, how can believers cooperate with God in evangelism? Here are four ways:

Identify with Christ. We can start by publicly (yet sensitively) acknowledging our life in Christ, declaring our spiritual commitments and convictions. We can also act with Christ-like love toward others and demonstrate integrity in our work and lifestyle. And we can identify with the people of God. That doesn't mean we have to endorse everything that other Christians do. But we accept and affirm that we are part of God's family (John 13:14–15; 17:14–19; Phil. 3:17).

Proclaim the gospel. Jesus preached repentance and the forgiveness of sins. Similarly, He asks us to verbally communicate the gospel message to our relatives, friends, and coworkers. Naturally, we must avoid preaching more than we practice. However, evangelism demands more than a "silent witness." As important as it is, our lives alone are not enough to guide people toward Christ's work for them. We must also provide information that presents Christ's message clearly and persuasively (Matt. 4:17; Col. 1:26–29).

Appeal for a decision. God gives people a choice to accept or reject His salvation offer. Therefore, as the Spirit gives us opportunity, we should present the gospel and then ask the person to decide what to do with Jesus (2 Cor. 5:18–20). For instance: "Is there any reason why you can't give yourself to Jesus Christ and accept the work that He has done for you?" We can act as Christ's ambassadors, appealing to others to accept His gift of new life.

In a way we're like midwives, carefully assisting in a new birth. Obviously, timing is crucial. To try to force premature delivery by high-pressure tactics and insistence on a decision only produces hostility, sometimes even rejection. It can create lasting wounds that close people's minds to the gospel.

Nurture and train new believers. We can continue to work with the Spirit to help new Christians get established in their faith. As a mother nurtures her newborn child, so we can nurture a baby believer (1 Thess. 2:7–8; 2 Tim. 2:2). We can assist the person in resisting temptation, developing new values, building relationships with other Christians, and gaining insight into the Bible. We can invite the "newborn" to pray with us, discuss God's Word, and worship the Lord.

Evangelism, then, is a cooperative effort between the Holy Spirit and those of us who follow Christ. As we interact with our associates, we should consider: How is the Spirit working in this person, and how can I contribute to the process? We can act like farmers, sometimes sowing new seeds, other times watering what someone else has planted. Occasionally we must root out an offensive weed left by someone else. But always our objective should be to reap a harvest to the glory of God (see John 4:34–38; 1 Cor. 3:5–7). ◆

What is the gospel we are called to proclaim? See Luke 7:22.

How you do your job affects your coworkers' attitude toward your witness. See "Your 'Workstyle,'" Titus 2:9–10.

A WOMAN IN LABOR

CONSIDER THIS 16:21–22 An alternative translation to *sorrow* (v. 21) is "pain." There were few options available to first-century women for pain relief during labor. Since births took place at home, all of the disciples had probably heard a woman scream out in pain while giving birth.

As in most undeveloped countries today, childbearing in biblical times was often fatal for the child, the mother, or both. Many pagan women sought help from their gods, along with special charms, to protect them during pregnancy and delivery.

So Jesus was using a graphic metaphor by comparing the coming "sorrow" of His followers with that of a woman in labor. He was indicating that their pain could not be avoided. But He did give them a hope: He promised that they would see Him again, and when they did their joy would be as great as a woman whose baby has finally been delivered safely.

Do you live with the hope of seeing Jesus, even as you confront the pain of this world?

17Then *some* of His disciples said among themselves, "What is this that He says to us, 'A little while, and you will not see Me; and again a little while, and you will see Me'; and, 'because I go to the Father'?" 18They said therefore, "What is this that He says, 'A little while'? We do not know what He is saying."

19Now Jesus knew that they desired to ask Him, and He said to them, "Are you inquiring among yourselves about what I said, 'A little while, and you will not see Me; and again a little while, and you will see Me'? 20Most assuredly, I say to you that you will weep and lament, but the world will rejoice; and you will be sorrowful, but your sorrow **16:21–22** will be turned into joy. 21A woman, when she is in labor, has sorrow because her hour has come; but as soon as she has given birth to the child, she no longer remembers the anguish, for joy that a human being has been born into the world. 22Therefore you now have sorrow; but I will see you again and your heart will rejoice, and your joy no one will take from you.

23"And in that day you will ask Me nothing. Most assuredly, I say to you, whatever you ask the Father in My name He will give you. 24Until now you have asked nothing in My name. Ask, and you will receive, that your joy may be full.

25"These things I have spoken to you in figurative language; but the time is coming when I will no longer speak to you in figurative language, but I will tell you plainly about the Father. 26In that day you will ask in My name, and I do not say to you that I shall pray the Father for you; 27for the Father Himself loves you, because you have loved Me, and have believed that I came forth from God. 28I came forth from the Father and have come into the world. Again, I leave the world and go to the Father."

29His disciples said to Him, "See, now You are speaking plainly, and using no figure of speech! 30Now we are sure that You know all things, and have no need that anyone should question You. By this we believe that You came forth from God."

31Jesus answered them, "Do you now believe? 32Indeed the hour is coming, yes, has now come, that you will be scattered, each to his own, and will leave Me alone. And yet I am not alone, because the Father is with Me. 33These things I have spoken to you, that in Me you may have peace. In the world you willᵃ have tribulation; but be of good cheer, I have overcome the world."

16:33 ᵃNU-Text and M-Text omit *will*.

CHAPTER 17

Jesus Prays for His Followers Then

17:1

¹Jesus spoke these words, lifted up His eyes to heaven, and said: "Father, the hour has come. Glorify Your Son, that Your Son also may glorify You, ²as You have given Him authority over all flesh, that He shouldᵃ give eternal life to as many as You have given Him. ³And this is eternal life, that they may know You, the only true God, and Jesus Christ whom You have sent. ⁴I have glorified You on the earth. I have finished the work which You have given Me to do. ⁵And now, O Father, glorify Me together with Yourself, with the glory which I had with You before the world was.

⁶"I have manifested Your name to the men whom You have given Me out of the world. They were Yours, You gave them to Me, and they have kept Your word. ⁷Now they have known that all things which You have given Me are from You. ⁸For I have given to them the words which You have given Me; and they have received *them,* and have known surely that I came forth from You; and they have believed that You sent Me.

⁹"I pray for them. I do not pray for the world but for those whom You have given Me, for they are Yours. ¹⁰And all Mine are Yours, and Yours are Mine, and I am glorified in them. ¹¹Now I am no longer in the world, but these are in the world, and I come to You. Holy Father, keep through Your name those whom You have given Me,ᵃ that they may be one as We *are.* ¹²While I was with them in the world,ᵃ I kept them in Your name. Those whom You gave Me I have kept;ᵇ and none of them is lost except the son of perdition, that the Scripture might be fulfilled. ¹³But now I come to You, and these things I speak in the world, that they may have My joy fulfilled in themselves. ¹⁴I have given them Your word; and the world has hated them because they are not of the world, just as I am not of the world. ¹⁵I do not pray that You should take them out of the world, but that You should keep them from the evil one. ¹⁶They are not of the world, just as I am not of the world. ¹⁷Sanctify them by

(Bible text continued on page 389)

17:2 ᵃM-Text reads shall.   17:11 ᵃNU-Text and M-Text read keep them through Your name which You have given Me.   17:12 ᵃNU-Text omits in the world.   ᵇNU-Text reads in Your name which You gave Me. And I guarded them; (or it;).

"**I** DO NOT PRAY THAT YOU SHOULD TAKE THEM OUT OF THE WORLD. . . ." —John 17:15

Gethsemane

A CLOSER LOOK 17:1 *Jesus' high priestly prayer recorded in this chapter was probably said in a familiar place of work. See "Praying in a Workplace," Matt. 26:36.*

CALLED INTO THE WORLD

Should followers of Christ withdraw from the world to set up their own exclusive communities or retreat from society into "Christian ghettos"? Not if they are to fulfill Christ's prayer in v. 18. Engagement, not isolation, is His desire.

Some early Christians sought refuge in the catacombs of Rome. But that practice was only temporary, and they were forced there only by the most extreme persecutions. Normally, they could be found actively participating in the society.

Actually, Scripture recognizes a tension between separation and involvement. Passages like Romans 12:2 and 1 Peter 1:14–16 urge us to pursue a distinctive, holy lifestyle. Our commitments, character, and conduct should contrast vividly with those of people who do not know or follow God. On the other hand, Jesus calls us to live and work side by side with those very same people. He sends us *into the world* to make an impact (see Matt. 5:13–16, and "Faith Impacts the World," Mark 16:15).

Naturally, that can lead to conflict. If our loyalty is given to Christ, we can expect tension with others who follow a different course. Whether we undergo mild teasing and insults or open hostility and even violence, "normal" Christianity involves conflict with the world to which we are called (see 2 Tim. 3:12; 1 Pet. 4:12–14). Fortunately, the New Testament gives us plenty of examples to follow:

Jesus. The Lord Himself came into the world to offer a new relationship with God. He didn't have to. He could have remained in His heavenly position. Yet He voluntarily left it all to die for us, and to deliver to a rebellious humanity God's offer of forgiveness, love, and acceptance (Phil. 2:5–8).

When Christ came into the world, His listeners showed initial interest. Yet gradually most of them turned against Him. Knowing full well the fate that awaited Him, He entered Jerusalem, ready to face persecution, arrest, and even death. His followers tried to divert Him (Mark 8:31–33), but He was determined to follow God's call into the world. Isolation and safety were not options.

Paul. The church's greatest messenger started out hating anyone who followed Jesus. Yet Christ Himself stopped him in his vengeful tracks and redirected his life to become a globe-trotting messenger of faith and forgiveness.

However, Paul's first days as a Christian were spent in an iso-lated "retreat" in Arabia. But this withdrawal lasted only for a time, and only so that Saul could emerge as Paul, *the apostle*. He crisscrossed the empire, bringing the gospel to dozens of cities and towns. These encounters led to numerous misunderstandings, deportations, arrests, physical abuse, and attempts on his life. Probably Paul sometimes longed for the safer, quieter days of his Arabian retreat. But once he responded to God's call to engage the world, there was no turning back. He also challenged others to live, work, and witness among the lost (1 Cor. 4:16–20).

Peter. Peter struggled throughout his life to break out of the separatist mentality he had grown up with. He didn't like the prospect of suffering and rejection, and at times took steps to forestall it (see Mark 8:31–38; Luke 22:54–62; John 18:10–11). He liked even less the idea of sharing God's good news of salvation with Samaritans and Gentiles.

But Christ kept calling Peter back to re-engage the world (for example, see Acts 10). In the end, he learned the necessity and the value of suffering (1 Pet. 4:1–2) and called others to do likewise (2:11–12).

Barnabas. A respected landowner, Barnabas enjoyed a relatively "safe" calling as a

(continued on next page)

Your truth. Your word is truth. [18]As You sent Me into the world, I also have sent them into the world. [19]And for their sakes I sanctify Myself, that they also may be sanctified by the truth.

17:18

Jesus Prays for His Followers Now

[20]"I do not pray for these alone, but also for those who will[a] believe in Me through their word; [21]that they all may be one, as You, Father, *are* in Me, and I in You; that they also may be one in Us, that the world may believe that You sent Me. [22]And the glory which You gave Me I have given them, that they may be one just as We are one: [23]I in them, and You in Me; that they may be made perfect in one, and that the world may know that You have sent Me, and have loved them as You have loved Me.

[24]"Father, I desire that they also whom You gave Me may be with Me where I am, that they may behold My glory which You have given Me; for You loved Me before the foundation of the world. [25]O righteous Father! The world has not known You, but I have known You; and these have known that You sent Me. [26]And I have declared to them Your name, and will declare *it,* that the love with which You loved Me may be in them, and I in them."

CHAPTER 18

Jesus Is Arrested

18:1–11

[1]When Jesus had spoken these words, He went out with His disciples over the Brook Kidron, where there was a garden, which He and His disciples entered. [2]And Judas, who betrayed Him, also knew the place; for Jesus often met there with His disciples. [3]Then Judas, having received a detachment *of troops,* and officers from the chief priests and Pharisees, came there with lanterns, torches, and weapons. [4]Jesus therefore, knowing all things that would come upon Him, went forward and said to them, "Whom are you seeking?"

[5]They answered Him, "Jesus of Nazareth."

Jesus said to them, "I am *He.*" And Judas, who betrayed Him, also stood with them. [6]Now when He said to them, "I am *He,*" they drew back and fell to the ground.

[7]Then He asked them again, "Whom are you seeking?"

And they said, "Jesus of Nazareth."

[8]Jesus answered, "I have told you that I am *He.* Therefore, if you seek Me, let these go their way," [9]that the saying might be fulfilled which He spoke, "Of those whom You gave Me I have lost none."

17:20 [a]NU-Text and M-Text omit will.

(continued from previous page)

leader of the infant church in Jerusalem. But he accepted an assignment to visit Antioch and investigate rumors of Gentile converts to the predominantly Jewish movement. Sure enough, he found that God was bringing all nations into the fellowship. So he sought out Paul, an unknown, to help him establish the new converts in the faith (Acts 11:19–26). Later, they traveled to Jerusalem to defend and extend this new "worldly" thrust in the growing work of God (Acts 15). ◆

THE BLESSING OF A CLEAN CONSCIENCE

CONSIDER THIS *18:1–11* **Would you feel free to welcome others to attempt to assassinate your character? Would you even help them? Jesus did. He had such a clean conscience and a secure trust in God that justice would ultimately prevail, and that His enemies could do no lasting harm, that He actually aided His accusers. He welcomed them (v. 4), identified Himself for them (vv. 5, 8), and even protected them from retaliation by His own loyalists (v. 11). Jesus demonstrated grace in the face of hostility.**

Jesus' innocence did not protect Him from suffering, pain, or death. But it gave Him a confidence rooted in a larger reality than life on earth. Because He answered to God's judgment (John 12:23–33; 14:1–4), He was free to suffer, even unjustly. He left justice up to God and did not resort to retaliation.

[10]Then Simon Peter, having a sword, drew it and struck the high priest's servant, and cut off his right ear. The servant's name was Malchus.

[11]So Jesus said to Peter, "Put your sword into the sheath. Shall I not drink the cup which My Father has given Me?"

[12]Then the detachment *of troops* and the captain and the officers of the Jews arrested Jesus and bound Him. [13]And they led Him away to Annas first, for he was the father-in-law of Caiaphas who was high priest that year. [14]Now it was Caiaphas who advised the Jews that it was expedient that one man should die for the people.

Peter Denies Knowing Jesus

[15]And Simon Peter followed Jesus, and so *did* another[a] disciple. Now that disciple was known to the high priest, and went with Jesus into the courtyard of the high priest. [16]But Peter stood at the door outside. Then the other disciple, who was known to the high priest, went out and spoke to her who kept the door, and brought Peter in. [17]Then the servant girl who kept the door said to Peter, "You are not also *one* of this Man's disciples, are you?"

He said, "I am not."

[18]Now the servants and officers who had made a fire of coals stood there, for it was cold, and they warmed themselves. And Peter stood with them and warmed himself.

[19]The high priest then asked Jesus about His disciples and His doctrine.

[20]Jesus answered him, "I spoke openly to the world. I always taught in synagogues and in the temple, where the Jews always meet,[a] and in secret I have said nothing. [21]Why do you ask Me? Ask those who have heard Me what I said to them. Indeed they know what I said."

[22]And when He had said these things, one of the officers who stood by struck Jesus with the palm of his hand, saying, "Do You answer the high priest like that?"

[23]Jesus answered him, "If I have spoken evil, bear witness of the evil; but if well, why do you strike Me?"

[24]Then Annas sent Him bound to Caiaphas the high priest.

[25]Now Simon Peter stood and warmed himself. Therefore they said to him, "You are not also *one* of His disciples, are you?"

He denied *it* and said, "I am not!"

[26]One of the servants of the high priest, a relative *of him* whose ear Peter cut off, said, "Did I not see you in the garden with Him?" [27]Peter then denied again; and immediately a rooster crowed.

> **"I SPOKE OPENLY TO THE WORLD. . . . AND IN SECRET I HAVE SAID NOTHING."**
> —John 18:20

18:15 [a]M-Text reads *the other.*   18:20 [a]NU-Text reads *where all the Jews meet.*

Jesus Is Taken to Pilate

28Then they led Jesus from Caiaphas to the Praetorium, and it was early morning. But they themselves did not go into the Praetorium, lest they should be defiled, but that they might eat the Passover. 29Pilate then went out to them and said, "What accusation do you bring against this Man?"

30They answered and said to him, "If He were not an evildoer, we would not have delivered Him up to you."

31Then Pilate said to them, "You take Him and judge Him according to your law."

Therefore the Jews said to him, "It is not lawful for us to put anyone to death," 32that the saying of Jesus might be fulfilled which He spoke, signifying by what death He would die.

33Then Pilate entered the Praetorium again, called Jesus, and said to Him, "Are You the King of the Jews?"

34Jesus answered him, "Are you speaking for yourself about this, or did others tell you this concerning Me?"

35Pilate answered, "Am I a Jew? Your own nation and the chief priests have delivered You to me. What have You done?"

36Jesus answered, "My kingdom is not of this world. If My kingdom were of this world, My servants would fight, so that I should not be delivered to the Jews; but now My kingdom is not from here."

18:37–38 37Pilate therefore said to Him, "Are You a king then?"

Jesus answered, "You say *rightly* that I am a king. For this cause I was born, and for this cause I have come into the world, that I should bear witness to the truth. Everyone who is of the truth hears My voice."

38Pilate said to Him, "What is truth?" And when he had said this, he went out again to the Jews, and said to them, "I find no fault in Him at all.

39"But you have a custom that I should release someone to you at the Passover. Do you therefore want me to release to you the King of the Jews?"

18:40 40Then they all cried again, saying, "Not this Man, but Barabbas!" Now Barabbas was a robber.

QUOTE UNQUOTE

CONSIDER THIS 18:37–38 *Pilate tossed the question to Jesus, "What is truth?" (v. 38). As an unbeliever, Pilate had no basis for measuring ultimate truth.*

To the non-believer, the person who sees no cosmos in chaos, we are all the victims of the darkness which surrounds our choices; we have lost our way; we do not know what is right and what is wrong; we cannot tell our left hand from our right. There is no meaning.

Madeleine L'Engle, *Walking On Water*, p. 27

• •

A Political Terrorist Goes Free

A CLOSER LOOK 18:40 *Barabbas was not only a robber (v. 40), he was a political terrorist, one of the* sicarii *("dagger-men") who assassinated Roman officials in the vain hope of driving them out of Palestine. Find out more at Mark 15:7 about how this revolutionary escaped the usual punishment of crucifixion.*

CHAPTER 19

DISCRIMINATION ON THE BASIS OF WEALTH

💡 **CONSIDER THIS** **The soldiers seemed**
19:1–6 **to enjoy mocking**
Christ (vv. 2–3). But they were also
mocking wealth and authority, per-
haps having lived and worked too
long under Rome's iron fist. The
crown of thorns was a grisly carica-
ture of the ultimate symbol of roy-
alty. But the purple robe was the gen-
uine item: the purple dye used to
make it was very costly and only the
very rich could afford it.

This incident reminds us that
wealth and its symbols can be used to
send many kinds of messages. Fre-
quently wealth is the starting point
for deciding who should be respected,
accepted, included, and honored, and
who should not. Scripture explicitly
states that sin lies at the root of such
judgments (James 2:1–9).

Do you judge people, in your
heart of hearts, by their possessions
and financial achievements? Do you
work hard at getting close to people
of position and wealth? Do your
friends come from many different
levels on the social and economic
ladder?

In Jesus' day, purple cloth was ranked in value with gold
and was important not only for adorning emperors and
temples but for tribute and international trade. See "The
Trade in Purple," Acts 16:14.

There is a marked contrast between how our culture
measures success and how God evaluates true success
and wealth. See "Success," John 3:30, and "Christians
and Money," 1 Tim. 6:7–19.

Pilate Sends Jesus to Be Crucified

💡 **19:1–6** [1]So then Pilate took Jesus and scourged *Him.* [2]And the soldiers twisted a crown of thorns and put *it* on His head, and they put on Him a purple robe. [3]Then they said,[a] "Hail, King of the Jews!" And they struck Him with their hands.

[4]Pilate then went out again, and said to them, "Behold, I am bringing Him out to you, that you may know that I find no fault in Him."

[5]Then Jesus came out, wearing the crown of thorns and the purple robe. And *Pilate* said to them, "Behold the Man!"

[6]Therefore, when the chief priests and officers saw Him, they cried out, saying, "Crucify *Him,* crucify *Him!*"

Pilate said to them, "You take Him and crucify *Him,* for I find no fault in Him."

[7]The Jews answered him, "We have a law, and according to our[a] law He ought to die, because He made Himself the Son of God."

[8]Therefore, when Pilate heard that saying, he was the more afraid, [9]and went again into the Praetorium, and said to Jesus, "Where are You from?" But Jesus gave him no answer.

💡 **19:10–11** [10]Then Pilate said to Him, "Are You not speaking to me? Do You not know that I have power to crucify You, and power to release You?"

[11]Jesus answered, "You could have no power at all against Me unless it had been given you from above. Therefore the one who delivered Me to you has the greater sin."

[12]From then on Pilate sought to release Him, but the Jews cried out, saying, "If you let this Man go, you are not Caesar's friend. Whoever makes himself a king speaks against Caesar."

[13]When Pilate therefore heard that saying, he brought Jesus out and sat down in the judgment seat in a place that is called *The* Pavement, but in Hebrew, Gabbatha. [14]Now it was the Preparation Day of the Passover, and about the sixth hour. And he said to the Jews, "Behold your King!"

[15]But they cried out, "Away with *Him,* away with *Him!* Crucify Him!"

Pilate said to them, "Shall I crucify your King?"

The chief priests answered, "We have no king but Caesar!"

[16]Then he delivered Him to them to be crucified. Then they took Jesus and led *Him* away.[a]

19:3 [a]NU-Text reads *And they came up to Him and said.* 19:7 [a]NU-Text reads *the law.*
19:16 [a]NU-Text omits *and led Him away.*

The Crucifixion

¹⁷And He, bearing His cross, went out to a place called *the Place* of a Skull, which is called in Hebrew, Golgotha, ¹⁸where they crucified Him, and two others with Him, one on either side, and Jesus in the center. ¹⁹Now Pilate wrote a title and put *it* on the cross. And the writing was:

JESUS OF NAZARETH, THE KING OF THE JEWS.

²⁰Then many of the Jews read this title, for the place where Jesus was crucified was near the city; and it was written in Hebrew, Greek, *and* Latin.

²¹Therefore the chief priests of the Jews said to Pilate, "Do not write, 'The King of the Jews,' but, 'He said, "I am the King of the Jews." '"

²²Pilate answered, "What I have written, I have written."

19:23–24 ²³Then the soldiers, when they had crucified Jesus, took His garments and made four parts, to each soldier a part, and also the tunic. Now the tunic was without seam, woven from the top in one piece. ²⁴They said therefore among themselves, "Let us not tear it, but cast lots for it, whose it shall be," that the Scripture might be fulfilled which says:

"They divided My garments among them,
And for My clothing they cast lots."ᵃ

Therefore the soldiers did these things.

19:25
see pg. 394 ²⁵Now there stood by the cross of Jesus His mother, and His mother's sister, Mary the *wife* of Clopas, and Mary Magdalene. ²⁶When Jesus therefore saw His mother, and the disciple whom He loved standing by, He said to His mother, "Woman, behold your son!" ²⁷Then He said to the disciple, "Behold your mother!" And from that hour that disciple took her to his own *home*.

19:24 ᵃPsalm 22:18

SEEING BEHIND POWER

CONSIDER THIS 19:10–11 Pilate assumed that he had more power than Jesus because he had authority to condemn Him to death (v. 10). But Jesus knew that all power ultimately comes from God, even the power of the state (v. 11; Rom. 13:1). Indeed, one of the reasons Jesus could submit to the injustices of His trial was that He was submitting to God's will (18:11). Pilate and those under him were merely exercising limited authority. Meanwhile, God's purposes were being fulfilled.

What sort of power do you have—in your work, at home, in your community? Do you recognize that your authority ultimately comes from God, and that you are ultimately accountable to Him for the use of that power?

. . . .

Success or Failure?

A CLOSER LOOK 19:23–24 *Would you consider your life a success if, at its conclusion, you had only the clothes on your back? That was the sum total of Jesus' wealth—and the soldiers took those away, leaving Him nothing (v. 24). For many of us, that kind of poverty would mark us as failures. "Jesus—A Homeless Man?" (Matt. 8:20) addresses the Lord's lack of earthly possessions and what that means for us today. As for the question* What is success? *see "Christians and Money," 1 Tim. 6:7–19.*

Submission to authority is never easy. Yet Scripture challenges believers to subject themselves to whatever governments they live under. See "Governmental Authority," Rom. 13:2.

John 19

28After this, Jesus, knowing*a* that all things were now accomplished, that the Scripture might be fulfilled, said, "I thirst!" 29Now a vessel full of sour wine was sitting there; and they filled a sponge with sour wine, put *it* on hyssop, and put *it* to His mouth. 30So when Jesus had received the sour wine, He said, "It is finished!" And bowing His head, He gave up His spirit.

31Therefore, because it was the Preparation *Day,* that the bodies should not remain on the cross on the Sabbath (for that Sabbath was a high day), the Jews asked Pilate that their legs might be broken, and *that* they might be taken away. 32Then the soldiers came and broke the legs of the first and of the other who was crucified with Him. 33But when they came to Jesus and saw that He was already dead, they did not break His legs. 34But one of the soldiers pierced His side with a spear, and immediately blood and water came out. 35And he who has seen has testified, and his testimony is true; and he knows that he is telling the truth, so that you may believe. 36For these things were done that the Scripture should be fulfilled, "Not *one* of His bones shall be broken."*a* 37And again another Scripture says, "They shall look on Him whom they pierced."*a*

19:28 *a*M-Text reads *seeing.*   19:36 *a*Exodus 12:46; Numbers 9:12; Psalm 34:20
19:37 *a*Zechariah 12:10

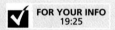

FOR YOUR INFO
19:25

THE WOMEN AROUND JESUS

Jesus went to His death attended by a loyal following of women who had stood by Him throughout His ministry (v. 25). Women played a major part in Jesus' life and work. It was a woman or women who . . .

- *Nurtured Him as He grew up (Luke 2:51)*
- *Traveled with Him and helped finance His ministry (Luke 8:1–3)*
- *Listened to Him teach (Luke 10:39)*
- *Were featured in His parables (Matt. 13:33; 24:41)*
- *Shared the good news that He was the Messiah (John 4:28–30)*
- *Offered hospitality to Him and His companions (Mark 1:29–31)*
- *Were treated by Him with respect and compassion (John 4:5–27; 11:32–33)*
- *Were healed by Him (Matt. 9:20–22; Luke 13:10–17)*

Jesus' Body Laid in Joseph's Tomb

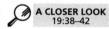
19:38–42

38After this, Joseph of Arimathea, being a disciple of Jesus, but secretly, for fear of the Jews, asked Pilate that he might take away the body of Jesus; and Pilate gave *him* permission. So he came and took the body of Jesus. 39And Nicodemus, who at first came to Jesus by night, also came, bringing a mixture of myrrh and aloes, about a hundred pounds. 40Then they took the body of Jesus, and bound it in strips of linen with the spices, as the custom of the Jews is to bury. 41Now in the place where He was crucified there was a garden, and in the garden a new tomb in which no one had yet been laid. 42So there they laid Jesus, because of the Jews' Preparation *Day,* for the tomb was nearby.

Jesus' Funeral

A CLOSER LOOK
19:38–42

Jesus' body was treated as a rich man's corpse might be—which could be due to the fact that rich people buried Him. See "A Burial Fit for a King," Mark 15:42—16:1.

- *Were praised by Him for their faith (Mark 7:24–30)*
- *Were commended by Him for their generosity (Mark 12:41–44)*
- *Worshiped Him and prepared His body for burial before His crucifixion (Matt. 26:6–13)*
- *Stood by Him at the cross (Matt. 27:55; John 19:25)*
- *Assisted in His burial (Mark 16:1; Luke 23:55—24:1)*
- *First saw Him resurrected (John 20:16)*
- *Went to tell the rest of His followers that He was risen from the dead (John 20:18)* ◆

Meet some of the individual women who followed Jesus at Luke 8:1–3.

How were first-century women involved in the spread of the gospel? See "Women and the Growth of Christianity," Phil. 4:3.

HE WHO HAS SEEN . . . KNOWS THAT HE IS TELLING THE TRUTH, SO THAT YOU MAY BELIEVE.
—**John 19:35**

SKEPTICS WELCOME

CONSIDER THIS
20:24–31

Have you ever struggled with doubts or troubling questions about Christ, the Christian faith, or the church? Do you sometimes feel that tough questions are not welcome or acceptable among believers?

Thomas (v. 24) was a classic skeptic. Even though he had traveled with Jesus and learned from His teaching for at least three years, he needed time, evidence, and personal convincing before he would accept the resurrection (vv. 25–26). But Jesus responded to his doubt by inviting him to check it all out. He presented Himself for Thomas' inspection (vv. 26–27) and did not chide him for wanting to be certain.

Jesus seeks to honor the mind and heart of every seeker or doubter. He knows that easily developed loyalties often lack staying power. By contrast, many tenacious people who probe the corners of their doubts and fears finally reach the truth—and faith in the *truth* is what Christ desires. He even promised that the Spirit would aid those who seek it (16:12–16).

The encounter with Thomas welcomes every skeptic to bring his or her doubts to God. He delights in hearing our arguments and questions.

If you're a skeptic when it comes to issues of faith and God, you may find some friends in the Old Testament books of Habakkuk, Job, and Psalms.

CHAPTER 20

The Resurrection

20:1–31

¹Now the first *day* of the week Mary Magdalene went to the tomb early, while it was still dark, and saw *that* the stone had been taken away from the tomb. ²Then she ran and came to Simon Peter, and to the other disciple, whom Jesus loved, and said to them, "They have taken away the Lord out of the tomb, and we do not know where they have laid Him."

³Peter therefore went out, and the other disciple, and were going to the tomb. ⁴So they both ran together, and the other disciple outran Peter and came to the tomb first. ⁵And he, stooping down and looking in, saw the linen cloths lying *there*; yet he did not go in. ⁶Then Simon Peter came, following him, and went into the tomb; and he saw the linen cloths lying *there,* ⁷and the handkerchief that had been around His head, not lying with the linen cloths, but folded together in a place by itself. ⁸Then the other disciple, who came to the tomb first, went in also; and he saw and believed. ⁹For as yet they did not know the Scripture, that He must rise again from the dead. ¹⁰Then the disciples went away again to their own homes.

Jesus Appears to Mary and the Disciples

¹¹But Mary stood outside by the tomb weeping, and as she wept she stooped down *and looked* into the tomb. ¹²And she saw two angels in white sitting, one at the head and the other at the feet, where the body of Jesus had lain. ¹³Then they said to her, "Woman, why are you weeping?"

She said to them, "Because they have taken away my Lord, and I do not know where they have laid Him."

¹⁴Now when she had said this, she turned around and saw Jesus standing *there,* and did not know that it was Jesus. ¹⁵Jesus said to her, "Woman, why are you weeping? Whom are you seeking?"

She, supposing Him to be the gardener, said to Him, "Sir, if You have carried Him away, tell me where You have laid Him, and I will take Him away."

¹⁶Jesus said to her, "Mary!"

The First Easter

A CLOSER LOOK
20:1–31

John's account of that first Easter Sunday (vv. 1–31) is part of an important body of evidence pointing to the resurrection as a historical fact. See "Evidence for the Resurrection—Jesus' Appearances," Mark 16:1–8.

She turned and said to Him,*ᵃ* "Rabboni!" (which is to say, Teacher).

¹⁷Jesus said to her, "Do not cling to Me, for I have not yet ascended to My Father; but go to My brethren and say to them, 'I am ascending to My Father and your Father, and *to* My God and your God.' "

¹⁸Mary Magdalene came and told the disciples that she had seen the Lord,*ᵃ* and *that* He had spoken these things to her.

¹⁹Then, the same day at evening, being the first *day* of the week, when the doors were shut where the disciples were assembled,*ᵃ* for fear of the Jews, Jesus came and stood in the midst, and said to them, "Peace *be* with you." ²⁰When He had said this, He showed them *His* hands and His side. Then the disciples were glad when they saw the Lord.

²¹So Jesus said to them again, "Peace to you! As the Father has sent Me, I also send you." ²²And when He had said this, He breathed on *them,* and said to them, "Receive the Holy Spirit. ²³If you forgive the sins of any, they are forgiven them; if you retain the *sins* of any, they are retained."

20:24–31 ²⁴Now Thomas, called the Twin, one of the twelve, was not with them when Jesus came. ²⁵The other disciples therefore said to him, "We have seen the Lord."

So he said to them, "Unless I see in His hands the print of the nails, and put my finger into the print of the nails, and put my hand into His side, I will not believe."

²⁶And after eight days His disciples were again inside, and Thomas with them. Jesus came, the doors being shut, and stood in the midst, and said, "Peace to you!" ²⁷Then He said to Thomas, "Reach your finger here, and look at My hands; and reach your hand *here,* and put *it* into My side. Do not be unbelieving, but believing."

²⁸And Thomas answered and said to Him, "My Lord and my God!"

²⁹Jesus said to him, "Thomas,*ᵃ* because you have seen Me, you have believed. Blessed *are* those who have not seen and *yet* have believed."

The Purpose of John's Gospel

20:30–31 ³⁰And truly Jesus did many other signs in the presence of His disciples, which are not written in this book; ³¹but these are written that you may believe that Jesus is the Christ, the Son of God, and that believing you may have life in His name.

THE PURPOSE OF JOHN'S GOSPEL

A CLOSER LOOK 20:30–31 *Whereas Luke tells his reader in the opening verses of Luke (1:1–4) and Acts (1:1–3) what those books are about and why he wrote them, John hangs the key to his Gospel at the back door of his narrative (John 20:30–31). That was a common practice in ancient writings. What we would call a preface was often placed at the end of a book, where it summarized the writer's purpose.*

John's "preface" tells us that he wanted his readers to find faith and life from his narrative. That's why he included seven sign miracles that show Jesus as the authentic, life-giving Son of God. See "The Seven Signs of John's Gospel" in the introduction to the book.

20:16 ᵃNU-Text adds *in Hebrew.*   20:18 ᵃNU-Text reads *disciples, "I have seen the Lord," . . .*   20:19 ᵃNU-Text omits *assembled.*   20:29 ᵃNU-Text and M-Text omit *Thomas.*

FORGIVENESS ABOUNDS

CONSIDER THIS
21:15–23

Do you ever feel hopeless regarding your faith? Do you doubt God's willingness to forgive you over and over again?

Peter (v. 15) might easily have felt that way. He had risen to a position of leadership among Jesus' followers. He had even been given the "keys of the kingdom" (Matt. 16:19). And he had positioned himself as the defender of Christ when Roman soldiers came to arrest Him (John 18:10). But when he felt the heat of a national trial, conviction, and death, Peter denied three times that he even knew Christ (18:15–18, 25–27) and afterward disappeared. What Jesus had predicted about him came true (John 13:31–38).

So when Jesus engaged Peter in a conversation on the shore (21:15–23), Peter might easily have felt that he was already disqualified from further service for the Lord. After all, as we would say, three strikes and you're out. But Jesus reconnected with Peter and called him to genuine love and the continuation of His work.

Second and third chances are not often available in families, communities, or workplaces. All you have to do is fail once too often, and you're gone. But Christ offers tangible love and boundless forgiveness—to those who own up to their failures and repent (Luke 7:47). Can we offer anything less to our coworkers, families, and friends?

Abundant forgiveness is something that Scripture stresses over and over for followers of Christ. See Matt. 18:21–22; Luke 17:3; Gal. 6:1.

CHAPTER 21

A Great Catch of Fish

¹After these things Jesus showed Himself again to the disciples at the Sea of Tiberias, and in this way He showed *Himself:* ²Simon Peter, Thomas called the Twin, Nathanael of Cana in Galilee, the *sons* of Zebedee, and two others of His disciples were together. ³Simon Peter said to them, "I am going fishing."

They said to him, "We are going with you also." They went out and immediately[a] got into the boat, and that night they caught nothing. ⁴But when the morning had now come, Jesus stood on the shore; yet the disciples did not know that it was Jesus. ⁵Then Jesus said to them, "Children, have you any food?"

They answered Him, "No."

⁶And He said to them, "Cast the net on the right side of the boat, and you will find *some.*" So they cast, and now they were not able to draw it in because of the multitude of fish.

⁷Therefore that disciple whom Jesus loved said to Peter, "It is the Lord!" Now when Simon Peter heard that it was the Lord, he put on *his* outer garment (for he had removed it), and plunged into the sea. ⁸But the other disciples came in the little boat (for they were not far from land, but about two hundred cubits), dragging the net with fish. ⁹Then, as soon as they had come to land, they saw a fire of coals there, and fish laid on it, and bread. ¹⁰Jesus said to them, "Bring some of the fish which you have just caught."

¹¹Simon Peter went up and dragged the net to land, full of large fish, one hundred and fifty-three; and although there were so many, the net was not broken. ¹²Jesus said to them, "Come *and* eat breakfast." Yet none of the disciples dared ask Him, "Who are You?"—knowing that it was the Lord. ¹³Jesus then came and took the bread and gave it to them, and likewise the fish.

¹⁴This *is* now the third time Jesus showed Himself to His disciples after He was raised from the dead.

Jesus Commissions Peter

21:15–23

¹⁵So when they had eaten breakfast, Jesus said to Simon Peter, "Simon, *son* of Jonah,[a] do you love Me more than these?"

He said to Him, "Yes, Lord; You know that I love You."

He said to him, "Feed My lambs."

¹⁶He said to him again a second time, "Simon, *son* of Jonah,[a] do you love Me?"

21:3 [a]NU-Text omits *immediately.*   21:15 [a]NU-Text reads *John.*   21:16 [a]NU-Text reads *John.*

398

He said to Him, "Yes, Lord; You know that I love You."

He said to him, "Tend My sheep."

¹⁷He said to him the third time, "Simon, *son* of Jonah,ᵃ do you love Me?" Peter was grieved because He said to him the third time, "Do you love Me?"

21:15–17 And he said to Him, "Lord, You know all things; You know that I love You."

Jesus said to him, "Feed My sheep. ¹⁸Most assuredly, I say to you, when you were younger, you girded yourself and walked where you wished; but when you are old, you will stretch out your hands, and another will gird you and carry *you* where you do not wish." ¹⁹This He spoke, signifying by what death he would glorify God. And when He had spoken this, He said to him, "Follow Me."

²⁰Then Peter, turning around, saw the disciple whom Jesus loved following, who also had leaned on His breast at the supper, and said, "Lord, who is the one who betrays You?" ²¹Peter, seeing him, said to Jesus, "But Lord, what *about* this man?"

²²Jesus said to him, "If I will that he remain till I come, what *is that* to you? You follow Me."

²³Then this saying went out among the brethren that this disciple would not die. Yet Jesus did not say to him that he would not die, but, "If I will that he remain till I come, what *is that* to you?"

²⁴This is the disciple who testifies of these things, and wrote these things; and we know that his testimony is true.

²⁵And there are also many other things that Jesus did, which if they were written one by one, I suppose that even the world itself could not contain the books that would be written. Amen.

21:17 ᵃNU-Text reads John.

The Meaning of Love

A CLOSER LOOK
21:15–17 *For a discussion of love and its actions see "Loving God Is More than Enthusiasm," 1 John 5:1–3.*

"**D**o you love Me? . . . Feed My sheep."
—John 21:17